INDIVIDUALISM AND THE JAPANESE

YAMAZAKI MASAKAZU

INDIVIDUALISM AND THE JAPANESE

An Alternative Approach to Cultural Comparison

Translated by Barbara Sugihara

Japan Echo Inc.

INDIVIDUALISM AND THE JAPANESE
An Alternative Approach to Cultural Comparison

©1994 by Yamazaki Masakazu
Translated by Barbara Sugihara
Translation ©1994 by Japan Echo Inc.

The two articles included in this book first appeared in Japanese
under the titles *"Nihon bunka no sekaisei"* and *"Aratamete kojinshugi to wa nanika"* in the spring and summer 1988 issues of the
quarterly journal *Asuteion*. They were subsequently included,
slightly revised, in *Nihon bunka to kojinshugi*, a hardback volume
published by Chūō Kōron Sha in 1990. This translation is based
on the latter version.

Published by Japan Echo Inc.
1-7-10 Moto Akasaka, Minato-ku, Tokyo 107, Japan

Designed by Takayama Graphics Inc.
Typeset by MoriAssociates
Printed in Japan by Takayama Inc.

ISBN 4-915226-05-0

Preface

Theories of Japanese culture abound both in Japan and abroad. Whether their exponents castigate or defend the country, however, they invariably attach great importance to clarifying the distinctive features of Japanese culture. The emphasis on cultural differences underlies every study, from Ruth Benedict's classic portrayal of Japanese culture as being based on a sense of shame to recent theories of the *ie* (household).

To a certain extent, this emphasis is an inevitable concomitant of any cultural study. A culture is a distinctive entity by virtue of differing from others, which brings tacit assumptions of comparison to any discussion of culture. For the sake of making the comparison clearer, many people are tempted to exaggerate the differences, leading to a focus on a given country's distinctive features at the expense of those characteristics it shares with other societies. In fact, however, commonalities are essential if comparisons are to be made.

A heavy object can be compared with a light one because both have weight, but comparing weight with breadth is

v

meaningless. The cultures of different countries can be contrasted because both are human cultures that can be assumed to share certain values. Past studies of individual cultures, however, have frequently forgotten to consider the basic nature of human culture, the values and qualities shared by all humankind.

This situation has occured primarily because the prototype of culture theory was developed in the West, by Westerners writing about other Western nations. Masterpieces like Wolfgang von Goethe's record of his travels in Italy and Alexis de Tocqueville's studies of American life are classic examples of writing predicated on a sense of homogeneity provided by the Western cultural background shared by the authors and the cultures they observed. The writers' intuitive understanding of Western culture obviated the need to question the nature of culture itself. Because the discrepancies were so slight, misgivings about emphasizing the differences between Germany and Italy or France and America were unnecessary.

Problems have arisen because the same attitude has been assumed in examining cultures like Japan's that differ far more widely from the observer's. The impossibility of grasping the homogeneous features intuitively should by rights have called for greater intellectual efforts to discover them. Viewing Japanese culture as based on a sense of shame in contrast to Western culture as characterized by feelings of guilt should have demanded a search for the common elements underlying both guilt and shame. The nature of human ethics should have been subjected to deeper philosophical, psychological, and sociological analysis. Adam Smith's *The Theory of Moral Sentiments* is but one piece of evidence that there is nothing uniquely Japanese about a sense of shame regulating the human conscience.

In this study I have tried neither to emphasize nor to deny the distinctiveness of Japanese culture. My intention has been to examine Japanese culture as one variation of human culture. This has been done in comparison with Western culture in Part I and in the context of an attempt at a universal theory of the fundamental nature of culture in Part II. I will be most gratified if this work serves not only to promote understanding of Japanese culture but also to deepen the reader's interest in the question of what culture itself actually is.

Not being a professional historian, I have relied on a great many specialists for historical facts. Insofar as possible clear acknowledgment of sources has been made in the relevant passage in the text; those omitted are listed in the bibliography at the end.

The two articles comprising this book were first carried in the quarterly journal *Asuteion* and subsequently published by Chūō Kōron Sha as part of a hardback volume titled *Nihon bunka to kojin shugi* (Japanese culture and individualism). I would like to express my sincere appreciation to the editors of both publications for the assistance they extended at the time. The present book owes much to the conscientious translation and editorial efforts of Barbara Sugihara. The deep understanding of Japan's culture, society, and language that she has brought to the project has resulted in a translation that is entirely to my satisfaction. In addition, I would like to express my deepest gratitude to President Mochida Takeshi and Maeda Keiichi of Japan Echo Inc. for the encouragement they have given me in planning the publication of this volume. My heartfelt appreciation also goes to the Suntory Foundation for providing the funds that made this project possible.

April 1994
Yamazaki Masakazu

Contents

CONTENTS

PART II
THE UNIVERSALITY OF GENTLE
INDIVIDUALISM

PART I
INDIVIDUALISM IN JAPANESE HISTORY

Chapter One:
Introduction

Over the past century the people and culture of Japan have been stereotyped in many ways. These stereotypes have sometimes found expression in ethnic jokes, such as those that depict Japanese tourists as round-shouldered, bespectacled camera toters and Japanese lecturers as always starting off with apologies and excuses. In a more serious vein, the various condemnations leveled against the Japanese at one time or another have characterized them as being everything from ominous people with unfathomable smiles to emotional hysterics.

Although such stereotypes may be on target to a degree, needless to say they generally exaggerate isolated aspects of reality. And regardless of how realities may change, stereotypes become firmly entrenched, taking on a life of their own. Of course it is not only the Japanese who are the brunt of such stereotypes; and ethnic jokes are enjoyed by people the world over. Human beings seem to like to give themselves a sense of security by forming simplistic notions about the cultures of other countries and the ethnic characteristics of other peoples.

Recently, however, the Japanese have been the target of stereotyping disguised as culture theory. As Japan's economy has grown and its status in the global community risen, the rest of the world has begun to take a more incisive and severe view of the country. Criticisms leveled in the context of trade friction are no longer limited to castigating Japan's economic activities but are escalating to attacks on the social and cultural traditions that underlie them. One notable example is the appalling remark attributed to a high-placed U.S. government official a few years back to the effect that Japanese culture itself will have to change if the trade imbalance between the two countries is ever to be rectified.

To make matters worse, the Japanese themselves have begun to squeeze their own culture into a stereotyped framework, adamantly insisting that it is immutable. When economic issues arise, "Japanese-style management" is proudly trotted out, with great emphasis laid on the group loyalties and cooperative spirit underlying it. Even less productively, friction over opening Japan's markets to foreign agricultural produce has been addressed with jingoistic sloganeering that touts rice as the symbol of Japanese culture and agriculture as the foundation of the nation—before making any attempt to find a rational, realistic solution to the problem.

Cross-cultural stereotypes are the product of fuzzy thinking. Reality is complex, and we become uneasy when we do not know how to interpret it, but we have neither the time nor the inclination to acquire a deep understanding of the other nations and ethnic groups sharing the globe. By singling out one aspect of a phenomenon, we can clarify our thoughts and put ourselves at ease. So we latch on to any pat explanation we hear, from ethnic jokes to high-sounding theories of culture.

The psychology that leads us to apply cultural stereotypes to ourselves personally or to our own nation or ethnic group seems more difficult to fathom; but this too is in fact a lazy person's device for getting through life simply and easily. In the drama of life, people find security in playing the roles they have chosen for themselves. Stereotyped role models provide them with a ready set of stage directions.

Our concept of masculinity illustrates this point. In the past, males in every country were educated to live and act in accordance with their society's idea of masculinity. Playing this role enabled them, for example, to endure grief in the face of tragedy. On the basis of parental teaching and the literature of their culture, they developed an image of the bearing and speech appropriate to men on such an occasion. In reproducing these, they unconsciously acted the part of the hero, thus consoling themselves.

Nobody finds it easy to determine the specific form that should be given to individual actions taken in response to the various situations faced amid the complexities of life. A simplistic concept of Japaneseness or of the Japanese cultural tradition makes it easy to choose a course of action. Particularly when confronting a crisis, people draw on history and legend to fortify themselves with stereotyped images of what the "typical" Japanese would do in the situation.

Such cultural stereotypes and preconceptions about ethnicity may be useful when the nation is handling a dispute, but employing them in this way runs the risk of forgetting about the diversity subsumed in the "typical" feature that has been selected and of unquestioningly accepting as the whole of reality something that is actually but one aspect of it. To use the example of masculinity again, people's reactions differ entirely depending on whether they hold an image of masculinity that focuses on physical strength, decisiveness, and roughness or on the sensitive, emotional side of the male nature that actually causes men to be far more bothered than women by trivialities and difficulties in interpersonal relations.

Swallowing preconceptions whole rather than subjecting reality to unprejudiced analysis can set a person's life on the wrong track. We observe ourselves living and form an image of self, but at the same time we unwittingly begin living in keeping with the image of self that we have created.

The same applies to theories of culture. The image of ethnicity that we construct will be reinforced and extended through our subsequent action, and, if mistaken, will lead us in directions we had not intended to take. We need to take a hard look at the frightening fact that a theory of culture is not merely a way of interpreting reality but also a standard for action that becomes, in turn, a framework for comprehending reality.

Culture is the collective character, or the pattern of living, that countless individuals have constructed together through a long, semiconscious historical process. The tremendous diversity and complexity resulting from this process means that people's image of a given culture differs entirely depending on the historical period that is focused on or the particular point in the diverse expanse of the whole that is chosen for emphasis. Special caution must be exercised when considering images òf culture and ethnicity and great care taken to avoid selecting a focal point arbitrarily.

The Pitfalls in Culture Theory

The way in which culture has thus far been associated with the concepts of nation and ethnic group—which have generally been developed through confrontation and conflict—has inclined people to consider cultural features within contexts of comparison and confrontation to an even greater extent than the characteristics of individuals, which are also sometimes defined in the context of struggle among individual members of a society. Today's economic friction and the world wars of the recent past demonstrate that attitudes of superiority and nationalistic self-assertion invariably accompany people's discussions of their own and other cultures. But when some reality, such as defeat in war, undermines this sense of superiority, extreme self-deprecation permeates the society, as happened in Japan after World War II.

Thus two dangerous tendencies inevitably accompany cultural theorizing. First, because cultural comparison lends itself to stressing differences rather than similarities, it tends to lead to overemphasizing a culture's unique attributes. In Japan's case, theories of culture have frequently gone hand in hand with racism and nationalism. Even in America, the idea of American "exceptionalism" has long been perpetuated, openly and otherwise. The Jews' seeing themselves as "the chosen people" and the Germans' idea of

7

ethnic mission derive from placing inordinate weight on the singularity of their own cultures and emphasizing their differences from other peoples. When inverted, however, such feelings of cultural mission are transformed into an inferiority complex. The Japanese poet Takamura Kōtarō (1883–1956) illustrates this dichotomy on the individual level. Although his first contact with Western culture, as a student in France, prompted him to write *Netsuke no kuni* (The land of *netsuke*) deprecating Japan's poverty and narrow-mindedness, he later became a fervent patriot who penned radical tributes to his country during World War II. For those who shun psychological complexities, dramatic contact with a different culture seems to elicit either inordinate self-confidence or excessive feelings of inferiority with regard to their native culture.

In either case, attributing singularity to a culture provides individuals with a strangely comforting prop when reflecting on their own existence and actions. The question of what I myself am, of what constitutes the essential nature of the self, is intrinsically a riddle that cannot be unraveled easily, but people tend to want an answer in order to live—and the easiest way to find one is to develop a sense of the group one belongs to and to express one's inner self in terms of it. The smaller the group and the more it stands in opposition to other groups, the clearer a person's apparent position in the world. The distortions in theories of culture are deeply rooted in this tragic weakness of human nature.

The second hazard of culture theories is what might be termed "cultural predestination" or cultural fundamentalism. Unlike mere systems and temporary rules, culture is sometimes viewed as having a life of its own that goes back to some definitive point of origin and is all but immutable because, like a living organism, if one part is altered the whole will perish.

When people consider culture to grow of its own accord, developing in conformity with the identity that has been programmed into it from the start, they quite naturally convince themselves that it cannot be intentionally altered by human effort. This leads to a sense of resignation that is comforting to lazy spirits. Having convinced themselves that today's difficult social problems are rooted in unchangeable cultural factors and therefore defy human remedy, such people can give them a sidelong glance and sit back with their hands folded. In fact, many recent political and economic issues could be resolved if only the effort were made, but they have been neglected because people are convinced that they are cultural matters.

Close examination reveals, however, that no culture is predestined to have certain characteristics. Of course a culture arises in a given place and is created by people constituting a specific group, by virtue of which it inevitably bears distinctive features. At the same time, however, different cultures influence each other, occasionally even fusing. There have been cases of cultures being transformed because of relocation, or of one ethnic group grafting its culture onto the myths of another by virtue of having already accepted the other group's religion at the time that its own myths were forming or by virtue of changing the religion of the group as a whole.

Culture has roots in the land only in a very limited metaphorical sense; it is in no way a rigid, unchanging organism that retains the same basic identity as long as it exists. Moreover, culture is certainly neither the mere physiological features of a people nor the automatic product of environmental influences. It is those special characteristics that people have actively created day by day and reinforced over the course of history, and thus is comparable to acquired customs and habits. Habits are admittedly difficult to change and exercise considerable control over people's day-to-day activities. Nevertheless, with effort and ingenuity habits can—and sometimes must—be changed.

Stereotyped Views of Japanese Culture

A couple of especially biased stereotypes have long held sway over theories of Japanese culture. The first overemphasizes Japan's agricultural tradition and the agrarian features of Japanese culture. Every ethnic group and culture has agricultural roots that continue to exert a strong influence, even in the case of modern industrial societies. Until very recently Germany, France, and even America were culturally at least as agrarian as Japan. But for some reason the Japanese tend to give special emphasis to the agrarian side of their culture even now that Japan is one of the world's leading industrial nations. Some popular generalizations include the idea that a great attachment to the land fatally weakens the Japanese people's enthusiasm for setting up businesses in other countries or that centuries of wet rice farming has made them placid vegetarians who lack the determination and enterprising spirit of meat-eating Westerners, who had to hunt their food. Some people go so far as to interpret the Japanese orientation toward other people and the strength of their tendency to imitate others as remnants of agricultural society, left over from the days when entire villages worked together to plant and harvest rice.

Mizuho no kuni, land of vigorous rice plants, is a poetic phrase that has been used to describe Japan since very ancient times. In the Edo period (1603–1868) the Tokugawa rulers stressed that agriculture was the foundation of the nation and established a social system based on four classes—warriors, farmers, artisans, and merchants, in descending order—thereby establishing the idea that agriculture is superior to industry and trade. This may account for the great sensitivity of agricultural issues in domestic political debate even today, as well as for the peculiar weight agricultural associations continue to have despite the drastic decline in the farm population and agriculture's tiny contribution to the gross national product. What is more, a surprising number of the urbanites who talk about literature and the arts exhibit a special nostalgia for rural society and the image of people whose lives are rooted in the soil. Discursive essays on the decadence and callousness of urban life and the "insecurity of rootless grass" have even become a sort of journalistic style. Japanese society as a whole clearly retains a sentimental attachment to agriculture, but I question the extent to which Japanese culture is essentially agrarian.

The second stereotype, closely related to the first, stresses group harmony and exceptionally close emotional ties within groups as unique features of Japanese society. The most easily understood form of this argument endeavors to explain the whole of Japanese society in terms of familism. Despite the presence of deep-rooted concepts of family and lineage in Europe and the direct control these institutions have exerted over the workings of Chinese and Indian society, the preconception that in Japan the family takes precedence over the individual frequently informs discussion of Japanese society in the absence of any precise comparison with other cultures.

From the Meiji era (1868–1912) down to the end of World War II, patriarchal familism did, indeed, weigh heavy on Japanese society, and preachers of enlightenment denounced it as a "feudal remnant" and a factor obstructing modernization. An authoritarian father and overly solicitous mother obstructing a youth's ego formation became a hackneyed literary theme. Literary circles long adhered to the tacit assumption that rivalry between father and son, on the one hand, and maudlin family love symbolized by the joint suicide of mother and child, on the other, were vestiges of ancient proclivities of Japanese society.

Closer examination, however, exposes this "wisdom" as facile at best, raising suspicions that people were projecting onto the past their dissatisfaction with the present. Since the Meiji era modernization and urbanization have rapidly nuclearized the Japanese family, a process that seems to have greatly strengthened such emotional bonds. The father heading a household in the loneliness of the city, separated from the extended family of the village, had to strengthen the authoritarian side of his character to shore up the family's morale and fortify it for the struggle for survival. By the same token, the mother took on stronger features of family guardian. Both roles were products of temporary historical circumstances more than of tradition. Failure to

realize this exemplifies culture theorists' hazardous inclination to regard present situations as permanent and to seek
explanations for present phenomena in past traditions.

Social scientists have recently conducted sophisticated
and precise studies of Japan's familistic groups. The American anthropologist Francis L. K. Hsu offers a penetrating
analysis based on careful observation of the Japanese *ie*
(household), pointing out its dual aspects as a "corporation"
and a "kin-tract." The Japanese scholars Kumon Shumpei,
Satō Seizaburō, and the late Murakami Yasusuke have
offered a new, singularly Japanese concept of the *ie* on the
basis of thoroughgoing cultural comparison. These new
approaches to the *ie* include noteworthy scholarly contri-
butions that clearly place them on a different level from the
concepts of simple familism assumed thus far.

These theories will be discussed in greater detail later;
for the present I would like to point out that, despite their
merits, both of these new approaches are problematic in that
they consider a unique *ie* structure to lie at the root of
Japanese culture, which is seen to revolve around a philosophy of harmonious cooperation and organizational
loyalty that is different from anything elsewhere in the
world. The cooperative philosophy these schemes describe
is not the group centeredness commonly found in popular
conceptions and clearly bears no relation to totalitarian sub-
mersion of the individual; on the contrary, it conveys the
polar opposite of closed blood ties and all-powerful patriarchalism. Nonetheless it is indubitably juxtaposed on the
modern Western concept of individualism.

Murakami, Kumon, and Satō, who have, significantly,
titled their study *Bunmei to shite no ie shakai* (*Ie* society

as a civilization), consider the characteristics of Japanese society to constitute a civilization, self-contained and discontinuous from other civilizations. The human relations underwriting this civilization are seen not as a variant of the relations found among individuals in the rest of the world but as the unique features of a civilization characterized by *aidagara* ("terms," or relations with others that are subsumed in a person's existence as such) or "contextualism." That is, Japanese harmonious cooperation and Western individualism are explained not as variations in degree but as differences between two opposing structures of human existence, disparities in the principles by which people live.

The distinctive structure of *ie* society is believed to have been instrumental in promoting Japan's modernization. The systems and customs that are regarded as keys to the success of modern Japanese business management—lifetime employment, seniority-based pay and promotion, company welfare plans, and enterprise unions—are seen as manifestations of fictive kin organizational principles rooted in traditional *ie* society. In positing that modern industrialization and the formation of capitalism need not be premised on Western individualism and may, in fact, be more effectively developed within *ie* society, these three scholars present a thesis that marks a revolutionary change from the folklore prevalent in the past.

Incisive though their analysis is, however, their attempt to set it up as an inclusive theory of Japanese culture leads me to suspect strongly that they are projecting their understanding of society in its present state onto analysis of the past. Features typical of *ie* society can be found in traditional

Japanese culture, to be sure, but although they may provide a broad foundation for modern corporate organization, I have reservations about claims that they are the salient attributes of Japanese culture. To establish that the contextualism of *ie* society is a principle of human existence comparable to individualism and that it is the basic structure creating a civilization demands clarification of two points. First, it must be demonstrated that individualism and contextualism do not merely represent variations in the degree to which some element is manifest but are, in fact, underwritten by different principles that reach down to the very roots of human existence. Second, this having been demonstrated, it must be proved that the structure of *ie* society is truly a core attribute of Japanese culture.

Precisely because *Bunmei to shite no ie shakai* is such an epochal work, I find these flaws very frustrating. I suspect that present-day Japanese society is so strongly imbued with an atmosphere of familial cooperation and that the preconception that this is our destiny has such a strong hold that even these distinguished scholars have been unconsciously influenced by it. To assess the validity of their theory of *ie* society, we must undertake an unbiased reexamination of Japanese social and cultural history.

Chapter Two:
Important Currents in Japanese Culture

ALTHOUGH various cases can be made for what constitutes the nucleus of Japanese culture and when it took shape, the implements and patterns of living that are generally considered typically Japanese first appeared as distinguishable cultural configurations from the Muromachi period (1392–1573) into the Edo period.[1]

To be sure, earlier periods produced invaluable treasures that have left an indelible mark on Japanese culture, among them the poetry of the *Man'yōshū*, compiled in the Nara period (710–94), and *Genji monogatari* (The tale of Genji), a novel depicting the court life of the Heian period (794–1192) in which it was written. At that stage in Japanese history, however, neither warriors nor merchants formed a distinctive social class, and the ethos and lifestyles that they would later represent did not yet exist. The warrior class came to the fore in the Kamakura period (1192–1333), when the prototypes of later political and legal systems took shape, but even then merchants and craftsmen had yet to become significant social forces. Not until the Muromachi period were all the classes constituting traditional Japanese society—nobles, warriors, peasants, merchants, and artisans —assembled on the stage, asserting themselves culturally and developing lifestyles of their own.

The Importance of Merchants and Artisans

Almost all the activities and cultural elements that we now associate most closely with Japan have been invented or developed since the Muromachi period. The tatami flooring, tokonoma alcove, and kakemono bearing a landscape painting that mark the typical Japanese-style room are all Muromachi creations. Prior to that, Japanese houses had wooden floors and people sat on straw cushions. A great many of the foods associated with Japanese cuisine also appeared in this period, when the techniques of Japanese cooking were systematized. In the late fourteenth century rules of etiquette were established that are still observed today.

Flower arrangement, tea ceremony, noh, and *kyōgen*— arts that Japan has placed in the arena of international exchange as the quintessence of its traditional culture— are all Muromachi products. Their development was given particular impetus by two prominent figures. In 1397, Shogun Ashikaga Yoshimitsu (1358–1408) built the Kinkakuji, the Golden Pavilion, in the hills of the Kitayama district of Kyoto. This exquisite retreat became a center where cultural leaders gathered to socialize, developing what has come to be known as Kitayama culture. Around the middle of the period, Shogun Ashikaga Yoshimasa stepped down from public life, retiring to his villa in Kyoto's Higashiyama section, where he devoted the remainder of his life, from 1473 to 1490, to patronizing the arts, inspiring new movements in theater, dance, painting, and architecture. His most famous architectural accomplishment was Ginkakuji, or the Silver Pavilion, which he had built on the site. Here he practiced the tea ceremony and entertained artists and other men of taste, both from the ruling class and from among the wealthy townspeople. *Yūgen* and *wabi*, aesthetic principles polished during these two eras, remain to this day the epitome of Japanese aesthetic ideals, giving this country's fine arts their celebrated aura of mystery and understatement.

Around the same time a nobleman named Ichijō Kanera (1402–81, also known as Ichijō Kaneyoshi), the foremost scholar of the day, annotated the *Genji monogatari*, establishing this ancient novel as a classic for all time and fixing the Heian period in the Japanese mind as an illustrious golden age to be looked back on with nostalgia and admiration. A good portion of what is now known about Heian court life and the culture of the aristocrats of the period is actually the result of rediscoveries made in the Muromachi period.

Also in this period Western cultural influences were added to those that had long been flowing from the Chinese mainland. The Japanese had their first glimpse of "red-haired, blue-eyed" Europeans, came in contact with the map of the world and the Roman alphabet, and learned of plants and animals in other parts of the world. They were also introduced to Christianity and received the benefits of European science and technology, ranging from guns and shipbuilding to Western medicine.

These cultural elements burgeoned even more spectacularly in the ensuing Momoyama period (1573–1603) and were further refined through the ingenuity and taste of Edo-period townspeople, thus nurturing on a national scale that which is now recognized as traditional Japanese culture. The Edo period not only gave birth to new art forms, such as the kabuki theater, *ukiyoe* prints, and *shamisen* music, but also contributed to the development of Japanese thought by reorganizing what had taken shape thus far and setting it down in writing. Particularly during the decades from 1688 to 1704, known as the Genroku era, publishing businesses targeting the masses came into their own. Their output included not only a great many literary works but also sober publications ranging from philosophical treatises and cultural works to business and farming manuals.

The traditional attitudes toward living commonly held by the Japanese, including their views of religion, politics, and economics, were formulated in part during the Kamakura period and to an even greater extent during the Muromachi and Momoyama periods. Articulated during the Edo period, they held sway over society until the dawn of the modern age.

Even this brief overview should make it clear that the core traditions of Japanese culture were by no means particularly agrarian or familistic. On the contrary, their strongly urban tone, commercial and industrial spirit, and fairly high degree of individualism makes them comparable to features that have characterized Western culture since the seventeenth century. Leaving aside for the moment fine arts and literature, the outer layer of culture, even the general customs of daily living confirm the deep respect the

Japanese had for commerce and industry and the high morale of the people engaged in these occupations.

This is not to deny that physiocratic attitudes produced a disdain of traders, just as they did in medieval Europe. The official ideology of the Edo period, in particular, relegated artisans and merchants to the lowest slots of the social structure, and Confucian scholars, such as Ogyū Sorai (1666–1728) openly scorned those who engaged in trade. The grounds justifying the value added through commercial activity are generally more difficult to comprehend than is the case with agricultural production, and the enormous profits that merchants frequently make have incurred resentment in societies the world over.

In view of this, Japanese traders had exceptionally high status and self-respect. Wealthy traders exercised amazingly powerful social leadership, particularly in the Muromachi and Momoyama periods. They associated with figures at the height of political power and the leading thinkers of the day, undertook a wide variety of public-welfare and cultural projects, and at times even organized semiautonomous mechanisms for governing their communities, as was done by the wealthy merchants in the trading port of Sakai. They were highly cultured, capable of strict ethical self-discipline, and had greater personal pride and self-assurance than even modern figures.

Their descendants, the townspeople of the Edo period, undaunted by the contempt in which they were held by the authorities, gained virtual control over society and vigorously asserted themselves culturally. Expressing their own taste in art and custom, as well as their own philosophy and worldview, they produced results that boldly made a case for their own point of view. A great many literary works appeared extolling merchants' raison d'être and their business philosophies. One was *Banmin tokuyō* (Right action for all), a treatise on morals by Suzuki Shōzō (1579–1655, also known as Suzuki Shōsan), a Zen priest who preached that each person's work, regardless of social class, was important and a road to enlightenment. Around 1740 Ishida Baigan (1685–1744) published *Tohimondō* (City and country dialogues). Baigan was the founder of the Shingaku movement, which exerted decisive influence on the morality of the common people, particularly the merchant class, in the Edo period. In *Tohimondō* he forcefully asserted the importance of each class to the proper functioning of society.

Mitsui Takafusa (1684–1748), an early head of the famed Mitsui merchant family, described the factors making and breaking wealthy commercial houses in his three-volume *Chōnin kōkenroku* (Observations on merchant life), in which he warned his heirs and descendents against unsound business practices and extravagant living, stressing that commercial prosperity depended on keeping human righteousness and profit making in balance, being thrifty, and working hard. A Confucian astronomer named Nishikawa Joken (1648–1724) produced a work titled *Chōnin bukuro* (Merchant's satchel; 1719). Taking the basic stance that all classes were equal, he enjoined townspeople to uphold the virtues of simplicity, thrift, modesty, and humility and to study disciplines that would enable them to practice moderation and strive for that which was reasonable and just.

In 1724 the Kaitokudō was established in Osaka. This

institution of higher learning, which drew students from both the samurai and merchant classes, numbered among its graduates Yamagata Bantō (1748–1821), a leading thinker of his time who distinguished himself both as a rice merchant and as a scholar. His rationalistic, materialistic approach to society and natural phenomena—very much a product of his studies at the Kaitokudō—was considerably in advance of his time and would later come to influence government, business, and educational thinking.

Good Faith and Sincerity

This social climate was underwritten by a concept of the public sphere of life dating back to the medieval period and by a feeling that it demanded loyalty and sincerity. In this case, the concept of the public realm transcended the family, business associations, and groups based on locality. It was instead a universalized, abstract human realm, very close in meaning to that of the word *tenka* as it was used in the late Muromachi period, that is, everything under heaven, or society at large. This perception of the world was widespread and must have been closely related to the growth of commerce.

Medieval Japanese considered the function of commerce to lie in the distribution of goods, and Shōzō spoke of commerce as "free trade in the world" and "free trade in the nation." He stated: "Without the samurai, society will lack rule; without the farmer, people will have nothing to eat; without the merchant, goods cannot be distributed throughout the world." Needless to say, distributing commodities means crossing regional boundaries and breaking through the closed barriers separating groups, which naturally gives rise to a universalistic image of the world. From an ethical standpoint trade demands honesty with respect to many different groups in addition to loyalty to a given group, in other words, honesty as an individual separate from the group.[2]

In his *Banmin tokuyō*, Shōzō articulated the merchant's ethic thus:

The merchant should first undergo training in the frame of mind for making profits. This means that all a person needs to do is live honestly and leave everything else to heaven. To the honest person, heaven will be generous and the buddhas and gods will provide protection. Disaster will not befall the honest person, who will have happiness and good fortune as a matter of course, will be loved and respected by the people, and will have all wishes granted in full measure. People who seek only to fulfill their own greedy desires, who discriminate between themselves and others, and who try to earn profits through deceitful dealings will bring down the wrath of heaven, meet with disasters, be hated by everyone, lose people's respect, and be thwarted at every turn. Status, wealth, and life span are all determined in a previous existence, and the desires of a person who selfishly wishes for fame and profits will not be fulfilled. On the contrary, one wrongdoing will follow another, flouting the way of heaven and bringing down divine punishment without fail. A person should take care that this does not happen, discarding selfish desires. If the merchant views his occupation as the role bestowed on him by heaven so that goods can be distributed freely throughout the country and, leaving his fate to heaven, makes honesty his prime policy in trade without thinking of profits, heaven will respond by fulfilling his every wish just as naturally as dried wood catches fire and water flows downhill.

For merchants in pre-modern Japan, honesty ranked with thrift as the greatest of virtues and was at times regarded as the highest moral principle, providing the basis even for thrift. According to Baigan, thrift was not a virtue having immediate, meaningful objectives in its own right; it was a way of strengthening the inner self and a means of returning people to "the honest state in which they were born." In his *Ken'yaku seikaron* (Essay on economical household management; 1744), Baigan taught: "When I speak of economizing, I am not talking only about clothing and other goods. My intention is to teach people to maintain a correct spirit and refrain from willful behavior in all aspects of living." Baigan awarded exactly the same status to sincerity as to other Confucian virtues, such as loyalty and filial piety. Not only did he not reduce sincerity to the other virtues, but at times he even seemed to place it above them.

In this regard, Shōzō warned that loyalty and filial piety frequently included utilitarian motivations and that in many cases service to lord or family was, in fact, a subconscious negotiation for a reward. Thus the purity of loyalty and filial piety as virtues depended on the sincerity of the individual. In *Mōanjō* (A staff to guide the blind), Shōzō taught that the practice of loyalty and filial piety could be truly virtuous only when accompanied by sincerity:

Devote yourselves to loyalty and filial piety. Sincerity is lost when a person is at the beck and call of reputation and profit. The sincere person is a rarity, even among those who are favored by their masters and serve as their close attendants. People think only of themselves and are preoccupied with their own desires. They should forget appearances, reflect on their actions, and make themselves aware that there is a virtue called sincerity. If a person is sincere, his children will be fond of him even though he may not think of himself as loving them. But even though he may treat another person's child affectionately, the child will not become fond of him if he lacks sincerity. He should be ashamed of himself.

It is difficult to maintain sincerity when following the dictates of loyalty and filial piety. Even the warrior who volunteers for the front lines and dies in battle does so in an effort to win fame and profit. The person seeking renown and increased territory complains that his stipend is too small or quarrels with others, trying to snatch up what they are aiming to get. Such people think nothing of righteousness and, following their own greedy instincts, continue behaving disgracefully. If they fulfilled the duties of loyalty in good faith, they would have no need to repent. If they were conscious of righteousness and acted bravely, they would no longer need to quarrel.

Needless to say, merchants are bent on making money, and the Japanese in general held little prejudice against profit seeking. Both Shōzō and Baigan were outspoken proponents of profit as the merchants' due payment for the contribution they made to society by distributing goods. "The trade of the merchants assists the empire.... Giving the harvest to the farmer is like the stipend of the *samurai*. Without the output of all the classes of the empire, how could it stand? The profit of the merchant too is a stipend permitted by the empire."[3] Such was the message of Baigan's *Tohimondō*. At the same time the merchants themselves seem to have held ethical values pertaining to the pursuit of profit and to money itself.

A puppet play by Chikamatsu Monzaemon (1653–1724) titled *Yamazaki Yojibei nebiki no kadomatsu* (The uprooted pine) describes a situation in which Yamazaki Yojibei, the son of a prominent merchant, is under house arrest, falsely charged with stabbing a man in a pleasure quarter; if the victim dies, Yojibei will be executed. It seems only natural and humane that the wealthy father use his fortune to save the young man's life, but although he loves his son, he refuses to put up the money, tearfully pouring out his feelings to a friend:

A samurai's child is reared by samurai parents and becomes a samurai himself because they teach him the warrior's code. A merchant's child is reared by merchant parents and becomes a merchant because they teach him the ways of commerce. A samurai seeks a fair name in disregard of profit, but a merchant, with no thought to his reputation, gathers profits and amasses a fortune. This is the way of life proper for each.... This trouble would never have arisen if only Yojibei had realized that money is so precious a treasure that it can even buy human lives. I am well aware that however much I begrudge spending my money, however much I hoard it, all that will be left me when I am dead is a single hempen shroud. But until I die I am bound to respect my gold and silver like the gods or Buddha himself—that is the way prescribed by Heaven for merchants. Supposing I gave still more money to that rogue, lavished it on him, even after he's been punished for his wicked extravagance. What dreadful punishment, what disasters would he then encounter! The more affectionately I think of him, the harder I find it to give him the money. I have the reputation of being a miser. Money is not the only thing I prize. I am loath to part even with dust and ashes. How could I not be reluctant to lose the life of my only son?[4]

Although this elderly merchant is clearly neither greedy nor heartless, he believes that money, treasure belonging to the public sphere of life, is not to be used for private purposes. He refers to respect for his fortune as the "way" and likens gold and silver to the gods or the Buddha, feeling that they are to be protected even if it means sacrificing the life of his son. This attitude, although probably exaggerated here, was not unusual. It provided the grounding for those who elevated the thought of theorists like Shōzō and Baigan into a business ethic.

Enthusiasm for Technological Innovation

An ethos stressing technology was nurtured among the masses and seems to have played an important part in enhancing the status of Japan's merchants and craftsmen, for merchants themselves were technicians who calculated money and weighed goods, and they frequently employed artisans and were on close terms with technicians in the fields of transportation and civil engineering.

The Confucian societies of the Asian continent have generally stressed abstract cultivation, disdaining practical, technical abilities, in line with the Confucian precept "A gentleman is not an implement." Those who wrote poetry and carefully observed etiquette were respected, but artisans, who made things with their hands, and merchants, who distributed goods, tended to be relegated to lower status. By contrast, before the pros and cons of moneymaking were brought into question Japan had a tradition of respect for physical labor—for work of a technical, practical nature—that transcended social class.

This probably relates closely to the political power reversal that occurred between the nobility and the warrior class as the latter's social status rose rapidly during the Kamakura period. The Chinese bureaucracy was always monopolized by literati chosen through the examination system, whose superiority to military administrators remained unshaken. In Japan, however, the warrior class was made up of people who were originally agricultural producers, land managers, and military technicians, whose technical skills enabled them to gain political power. Many of Japan's medieval warlords were instrumental in increasing production and promoting industry and were themselves proficient in civil engineering, architecture, and the law, and the peasants under their control had boundless enthusiasm for technical innovation and new projects.

The drive to raise income by breaking new ground for paddy fields, common to peasants and lords alike, dated back to the end of the Heian period—an entrepreneurial spirit that continued to grow in and after the Muromachi period.

Paralleling this were dramatic improvements in crop strains and agricultural techniques, particularly during the Edo period. In the seventeenth and eighteenth centuries many outstanding, intellectually oriented farmers emerged in villages throughout the nation. They undertook studies of agricultural techniques, producing commentaries that they began to publish widely. The *Nōgyō zensho* (Agricultural compendium) of Miyazaki Antei (1623–97, also known as Miyazaki Yasusada) was one of a succession of excellent agricultural treatises published around the turn of the eighteenth century. Tsukuba Hisaharu, a scholar of technological history, has described them as displaying attitudes that have much in common with modern scientific methods. They are based on experience, are verifiable, and make a rational attempt to generalize local experience and inquire after universal knowledge. This attitude was also applied to the cultivation of flowers in cities, so-called horticultural technology, which the ethnologist Nakao Sasuke has called the most advanced in the world, at least in the eighteenth century. Even today, developing improved varieties of chrysanthemums, azaleas, and morning glories is a popular pastime among the Japanese.

Up to now, standard interpretations have divided historical periods into stages—the age of hunters and gatherers, the agricultural period, the industrial age—and have usually considered a given society to have the characteristics associated with whatever stage it is in. As the terms "agrarian culture" and "industrial culture" indicate, the culture of a given society has been seen as a reflection of the basic structure of its economy. This view has not been limited to Marxist theorists but has been tacitly assumed by social scientists in general. If culture is the stance people take in life, the rhythm of their daily living, it is, of course, influenced by economics, but it must be kept in mind that the reverse is also possible.

For example, agriculture as a form of production affects the way people live, but at the same time, a people's way of life can be expected to determine the way agriculture is conducted. In some countries agriculture is characterized by a reverent submission to nature, by the eternal repetition of activities assimilated to the cycle of the seasons. In such societies daily life has a stable rhythm, continuity of tradition is valued, and the culture is apt to exhibit conservative resistance to sudden change. We must, however, be aware that this type of culture is not the inevitable product of agriculture and may not even be the result of the agricultural practices specific to a given country. The opposite may in fact be the case. It may be more reasonable to think in terms of this conservative way of life existing in the society beforehand and eventually giving the country's agriculture its bucolic features.

The great enthusiasm that Japanese peasants had for technical innovation and the alacrity with which they accepted changes in their way of living incline me to think that the latter was the case in Japan. If this is the attitude of modern progressivism and the psychology characteristic of industrial society, then it is no exaggeration to say that the Japanese lived the medieval period in a modern fashion and conducted agriculture in the spirit of the industrial age. In fact, the Japanese of the Muromachi period imitated and improved on the new science and technology introduced from the West with astonishing eagerness and skill. To relate one example, in 1543 a Portuguese ship arriving at the island of Tanegashima presented its lord with two guns. A local swordsmith was ordered to produce copies but had no idea how to go about it. Legend has it that in order to obtain the necessary technology he presented his daughter to the ship's captain. Only three decades later, however, guns were being produced in lots of several thousand and used as the main weapon in the battles of the warlord Oda Nobunaga (1534–82) for control of the nation.

The flat-bottomed sailing ships originally used by the Japanese were unsuited to navigating the high seas. The Portuguese arrived in galleons with keels that enabled them to traverse great distances. With amazing speed, the Japanese mastered the technologies for building such ships. In 1613 Hasekura Tsunenaga crossed the Pacific from Sendai to Mexico in a Western-style ship made entirely in Japan. Even after this long voyage the craft was seaworthy enough that the Spanish navy appropriated it as a warship.

The technologies imported were not, of course, limited to those used in manufacture. Sailing a ship also requires the technology for navigating it. A book on navigation written at the time recording questions and answers exchanged between a Japanese and a Western ship's captain bears testimony to the alacrity with which the seamen of the Muromachi period learned Western navigation. Insightful and meticulous, the questions posed are highly impressive even by today's standards. Western medicine was also introduced through very limited contacts with Dutch traders.

Gradually, however, it developed on its own. Eventually a physician named Hanaoka Seishū devised an anesthetic, performing the first surgical operation under general anesthesia in 1805, 40 years before ether came into use in the West.

Such technology assimilation and innovation seems to have been made possible by the high intellectual level and finely tuned cultural sense of the masses rather than by the abilities of a small elite. The ideas of standardization and production in matching sets have long been applied to the many items of daily living representative of Japan's traditional culture. For centuries, techniques to standardize parts and combine them in different ways have been applied to everything from tatami and building materials to matching dishes and the way cloth is cut for kimono. The idea of creating a whole by combining standardized parts that can be interchanged as necessary was perfected in modern America, but in a germinal form it has existed in Japan for a very long time.

Other Asian countries have also possessed the ability to make precision products and standardized goods. Individual items demonstrate high technological standards: the incomparably delicate, high-grade ceramics of China and Korea and the elaborate parts of the Western-style clocks in the palaces of China, for example. But Japan probably came closest to resembling modern Western societies because its technologies were not primarily the property of the court and a limited number of aristocrats but spread widely among the populace.

The sense for precision not only applied to visible objects but also extended to measuring the time that governed people's actions. The historian Tsunoyama Sakae has pointed out that in the Edo period many ways of telling time spread along with clocks and that awareness of time in units of minutes penetrated every class of society. He has noted the precision, to the minute, with which a traveling companion of the seventeenth-century haiku poet Matsuo Bashō recorded in his journal the time of their arrival at an inn or of an unexpected rainstorm. An exact sense of time and an ethic of being on time are important cultural foundations of modern industry. Their early establishment among the common people is a feature of Japanese society that seems to be rare in other Asian countries.

A culture of the masses that extended not only to science, technology, and the production of goods but also to every field of endeavor, from education to amusement, appeared early in Japanese history. Among the populace the custom of learning to read, write, and correspond by letter began far back in history. During the Muromachi period *ōrai-mono*, correspondence manuals that had first appeared in the Heian period, spread rapidly and widely, even among low-ranking warriors and merchants. The Edo period saw the development of *terakoya*, privately run schools that enabled not only samurai and merchant children but even those living in villages to receive the benefits of an elementary education.

In the area of amusement, the tea ceremony, for example, was a luxurious and exorbitantly expensive pastime. At the same time, however, powdered tea was whipped up and sold on street corners for a penny a bowl. In 1587, when a grand tea ceremony was held at Kitano Tenmangū shrine in Kyoto, the de facto ruler, Toyotomi Hideyoshi (1537–98) issued a proclamation permitting people to bring parched barley flour to the great garden party instead of powdered green tea so that even those who could not afford tea could learn the proprieties of the tea ceremony and enjoy the gathering.

A fad that appeared in the same period was gatherings to compose *renga*, or linked verse, the participants taking turns at linking couplets of five and seven syllables to form one long poem. This pastime, too, could be enjoyed by anyone, from a feudal lord down to the lowliest commoner. People who lacked the space to entertain at home would get together out of doors to enjoy this literary socializing.

Noh, which was monopolized by high-ranking samurai in the Edo period, had been a theatrical form for the public at large in the early Muromachi period, when it was perfected by Zeami Motokiyo (1363–1443). His *Fūshi kaden* (The transmission of the flower of acting style) indicates that noh actors of his day had to perform before audiences drawn from a broad spectrum of the public and racked their brains to devise ways of imparting the same enjoyment to people of different classes and different tastes.

One ideal of noh is to win the love and respect of the common people, and to perform in a way that would capture the interest of people unable to appreciate the refinements of the art was a lesson taught by Zeami, who at the same time devoted his life to the pursuit of the highest aesthetic principles. When the Tokugawa shogunate appropriated noh as its official theater in the Edo period, kabuki and bunraku puppet theater developed in its stead, enjoying tremendous popularity as entertainments for the public at large.

Cities and the Tradition of Socializing

Remarkably early urbanization provided a backdrop for this fluorescence of trade and industry and the establishment of mass culture in premodern Japan. Of course any number of populous cities existed in other parts of the world, and since antiquity a prodigious number of cities have been built on a grand scale and embellished with monumental architecture. But not until relatively recent times have cities arisen that not only have large populations and cover extensive areas but also contain a wide diversity of human types, each asserting its cultural individuality. The definitive qualifications making an urban area a city in the strictest sense of the word are that its citizenry include a diversity of individual types and, as a whole, possess urban attitudes.

By this measure, Kyoto in the first half of the present millennium was probably one of the world's earliest real cities. Founded in the Heian period as a political center, it was the seat of the court. Eventually, however, the rising warrior class threatened the power of the nobility. In the Muromachi period the warriors coexisted with merchants and craftsmen, each group becoming a force within the city. The early fourteenth century writer Yoshida Kenkō's *Tsurezuregusa* (Essays in idleness) gives a glimpse of the many types of people coming and going in the Kyoto of his time and some idea of the different values and lifestyles that they were beginning to assert. This work suggests the sense of themselves as urbanites—an awareness distinct from the prevailing class consciousness—that was beginning to take shape, at least among intellectuals.

36

According to Kenkō, urbanites are people of good taste, and people of good taste are those who, in all things, have the grace to remain detached in their contact with that which is unusual or interesting. Viewing from a distance whatever excites the human heart, whether the moon or flowers or a festival, constitutes the superior sensibility of the urbanite. The country bumpkin, by contrast, pushes himself right up against anything and everything, getting as close as possible to whatever catches his fancy. If flowers are in bloom, the boor breaks off a branch and takes it home; if snow falls, the yokel walks on it and leaves footprints; if there is clear water, the bumpkin feels compelled to stick a hand in and cloud it. With an urbanite's pride, Kenkō wrote disdainfully of country people:

Such people have a very peculiar manner of watching the Kamo Festival. "The procession's awfully late," they say. "There's no point waiting in the stands for it to come." They go off then to a shack behind the stands where they drink and eat, play *go* or backgammon, leaving somebody in the stands to warn them. When he cries, "It's passing now!" each of them dashes out in wild consternation, struggling to be first back into the stands. They all but fall from their perches as they push out the blinds and press against one another for a better look, staring at the scene, determined not to miss a thing. They comment on everything that goes by, with cries of "Look at this! Look at that!" When the procession has passed, they scramble down, saying "We'll be back for the next one." All they are interested in is what they can see.

People from the capital, the better sort, doze during

the processions, hardly looking at all. Young underlings are constantly moving about, performing their masters' errands, and persons in attendance, seated behind, never stretch forward in an unseemly manner. No one is intent on seeing the procession at all costs.[5]

Until then, superiority or inferiority of status, the relations among classes, had been the only criterion people had possessed for making value distinctions among themselves. The yardstick of rank was whether a person was noble or commoner, lord or peasant. In the Muromachi period, however, a new standard seems to have come into play, the distinction between urbanite and country dweller. Literary works of the period extol new, urban attitudes, that is, the pride of the Kyotoite. With the comic satire of a good *kyōgen*, *Sue hirogari*, a well-known play of this genre, depicts a retainer of a country feudal lord being taunted by city commoners.

Of course the industry that fundamentally sustained Japanese society from the thirteenth through the late nineteenth century was agriculture, and the principles of this agricultural society may have created the framework of the political system. The city, however, probably played a greater role than has previously been assumed in shaping the Japanese national character and in forming the features of Japanese culture. At the least, although agriculture was important throughout the world during those centuries, the early establishment of urban attitudes was, to a considerable degree, a distinctively Japanese phenomenon.

Japanese cities have never been isolated from their surrounding rural communities, a fact that has allowed uninterrupted cultural exchange between town and country. In contrast to cities in China and Europe, Japanese cities have never been encircled by high walls that clearly demarcate inside from outside. Since people could come and go at will, they imbibed one another's cultures. Zeami's discussions of noh indicate that he saw himself as one who had left the countryside to go to Kyoto, where he established a style of his own, polished under the sharp eyes of urbanites, which he then took back to the villages to educate the peasantry in artistic taste.

A wide variety of social gatherings, similar to the salons of eighteenth-century Europe, were in vogue in the Kyoto of Zeami's time. Warriors, priests, nobles, and wealthy merchants gathered at aristocrats' mansions and the leading Zen temples to create poetry, view paintings, enjoy tea, and nurture friendships. As I will discuss later, Japanese literature and fine arts had, in fact, been the products—and the sustenance—of aristocratic socializing since the Heian period. This type of socializing reached a peak in the Muromachi period and set the salient features of culture thereafter. To qualify as a gentleman among the townspeople of the Genroku era, for example, one had to engage in social activities revolving around the performing arts, and in this milieu flowered a wide variety of arts, ranging from music and dance to parodic versifying. Even many members of the samurai class found their raison d'être in the literary and artistic salons of Edo, feeling more at home there than in their feudal domains.

Chapter Three:
Individuality and Artistic Expression

Wealthy Japanese merchants of the Muromachi and Momoyama periods probably had few parallels in the rest of the world in that, in addition to being superlative businessmen, each was an individual with a rich inner life, a possessor of artistic accomplishments and scholarship who exhibited taste and talent in daily living.

These merchants instituted a wide variety of business projects and amassed fortunes, but they also contributed in many ways to creating the cultural legacy that still exists today. In serving as patrons of scholars and artists they resembled the wealthy merchants of the European Renaissance. But they also produced from their own ranks a number of outstanding cultural leaders.

Japan's medieval merchants not only brimmed with a spirit of adventure and creativity in business but also used their own eyes and hands to give their inner world tangible artistic expression. These merchants' orientation toward individuality and respect for individual tastes and talents grew out of a long cultural tradition. The cultural leaders of the

Muromachi and Momoyama periods also enthusiastically revived classical works, being drawn to those that depicted the highly individualistic spirit of the Heian court. Of course the Heian aristocrats, like aristocrats the world over, did not respect manual work. As in any classical age, the spirit of the court held a single, ideal aesthetic to be absolute, tending to wariness of anything different, anything expressing heterodox values. Although there was no active orientation toward individuality of either taste or talent, an attachment to the private world and a strong interest in daily life close to the individual had unmistakable prominence in Heian court culture.

The Private World in Japanese Literature

The best-known works of Japanese classical literature include poetry collections and novels of courtly love like the *Genji monogatari* and the *Ise monogatari* (Tales of Ise). Modern research has revealed these to be the world's earliest novels, meaning that they portray a purely private world. Their themes center on the romantic feelings of numerous couples, confessions of these individuals' innermost joys and sorrows, and detailed scenes of the life around them. The characters are life-size people with ordinary human psyches, not heroes invested with superhuman abilities and ideals; they are placed in a world that is no larger than the space of ordinary living, not on the stage of mythological giants, where peoples and clans rise and fall in political struggle and battle.

The main themes in the early literature of every ethnic

group are set in the realm of the tribal community; they are not concerned with the self. Literature long remained confined to tales of ethnic heroes and mythological superhuman beings, not only in ancient Greece but also in medieval Europe. Even love songs merely lauded the ideal of a universalized love set on an abstract stage, unrelated to raw human passions. The hero either exemplified a religious precept or embodied an emotion.

Japan, too, has rudimentary epic poetry and an outstanding ethnic literature, such as the *Kojiki* (Records of ancient matters) and the *Nihon shoki* (Chronicle of Japan). Japanese literature is distinctive, however, in that shortly after these works were compiled the Japanese were already writing novels, focusing on the subtle psychology of the individual and observing the delicate nuances of ordinary life. The leading characters in *Genji monogatari* and *Ise monogatari* bear no relation to ethnic heroes and have little connection to the ideals and abilities involved in ruling the nation. On the contrary, they are people who have been unlucky in the world of politics—the disappointed prince, the figure who has early given up struggling in the public realm. They do not even feel anger over their political fate, consoling themselves with romantic adventures with lovely ladies as if seeking compensation for having given up. And the women who appear as their counterparts, far from being magnificent goddesses, are real-life people tormented by jealousy, disappointment, and despondency.

A great many essays and diaries have also contributed significantly to defining the characteristics of Japanese literature. These begin with well-known works from the Heian court—the *Makura no sōshi* (Pillow book) of Sei Shōnagon, the *Murasaki Shikibu nikki* (Diary of Lady Murasaki Shikibu), and the *Tosa nikki* (Tosa diary)—and continue down through the Kamakura and early Muromachi periods with such collections of essays as *Hōjōki* (An account of my hut) and *Tsurezuregusa*. In general, diaries and essays are eminently the product of the individual heart and, needless to say, deal primarily with private life.

In the works considered great in Japan, the author's interest is concentrated on near-at-hand natural phenomena, human affairs, customs, and fads. These works are lyrical rather than epic. There are some medieval diaries that record public life, giving us a valuable historical record of contemporary events, but the literary works that the Japanese have traditionally read with the greatest pleasure and kept alive as classics are centered on confessions of private emotion. I might add that even modern journalism has created an essay genre that avoids outright discussion of social and political issues, rambling on instead about the pros and cons of individual aesthetics.

Impressive, too, is the overwhelming importance attributed to tanka and haiku, short lyric poetic forms. Such verses, created in prodigious numbers since ancient times, have been of far greater influence than the epic poetry of such works as the *Kojiki*. A classic is not simply a masterpiece written long ago; it provides a framework for the sensibilities of later generations and is repeatedly revived as the thematic matrix of new works. In Japan, short poems have fulfilled this role more than novels. Through the technique of *honka-dori*—in which a poem allusively echos an earlier one, simultaneously adding the significance of the previous poem to the new one and giving the old elements fresh meaning—the poetry of one age has provided the basis for that of a later time. Short poems have also supplied a wealth of ideas for stories and plays.

The Japanese people have made these distinctive lyric poems a part of the ethnic memory, memorizing them for emotional nourishment as well as sheer enjoyment. This genre probably boasts more poets than any other in the world, for men and women of every age and status have traditionally marked the various junctures in their lives by creating tanka and haiku expressing their personal feelings. This broad-based mass interest in the inner life deserves study as a sociological phenomenon.

A distinctive feature of Japanese classical theater forms like noh and kabuki is that the protagonist is almost always a private person unrelated to the world of organizations and officialdom. Many of the main figures in noh are losers in politics and war who no longer harbor any desire to take revenge on their enemies. They have already reverted to being lone, naked human beings, pouring out grief rather than anger and wandering in search of repose for their anguished souls. But the dominant themes of noh are romance and familial love, the emotions of a woman longing after a man or heartsick for a dead child. Zeami, who brought noh to perfection, made the beauty of *yūgen* his artistic ideal. The term *yūgen* as he used it refers to ethereal feminine grace and charm, such as that seen in the women of the Heian court. Noh idealizes feminine beauty and focuses on the feminine aspects of human emotion, which may make it a rare theatrical form in history as a whole.

Similarly, the central themes in kabuki are romance and family affection; neither epic heroes nor nobles, aristocrats, and their ilk are ever the protagonists. Even when an occasional hero appears as a national savior, as in Chikamatsu's play *Kokusen'ya kassen* (The battles of Coxinga), his political activities serve only to shape the outer frame of the plot. The main point of the play lies always in scenes portraying affection between husband and wife or parent and child. Even when national political strife sets the stage for the drama, the real hero is usually an insignificant man sacrificed to this cause and his unfortunate wife and children, as in Takeda Izumo's *Sugawara denju tenarai kagami* (Sugawara and the secrets of calligraphy). In the so-called domestic plays, which account for the majority of popular productions, the main theme is limited to the everyday joys and sorrows of people of the marketplace, concentrating particularly on the conflict between romantic love and familial affection. The young protagonist lacks not only political ideals but also, apparently, any desire to go into business or ambition to make a name for himself. He spends his time suffering from love for a prostitute, writhing under familial fetters, and proceeding down the path to joint suicide with his lover.

Japanese theater has no counterparts of the *Oedipus* of Greek drama or Shakespeare's *Hamlet* and *Macbeth*. Interestingly, however, both noh and kabuki nonetheless possess the means for magnificent stylization in the theatrical techniques they employ to make small figures appear large. The Japanese do not seem to be incapable of seeing human beings as grand entities; on the contrary, they appear to be rich in the ability to see greatness in private individuals whose lives are close to their own.

True epics having the nation as their stage and the rise

and fall of groups as their theme have appeared in Japanese literature only in war chronicles, such as the *Heike monogatari* (Tale of the Heike) and the *Taiheiki* (Chronicle of the great peace). They were compiled during the turbulent era of civil strife spanning the Kamakura period and the period of the Northern and Southern Courts (1333–92), the age in which *ie* society was being developed under the leadership of warriors from the eastern regions.

In these tales the true protagonist is clearly the *ie* itself, along with the valiant heroes who symbolize it. Japanese interest in the *ie* undoubtedly rose dramatically in this period. What is more, these tales of battle have influenced subsequent literature and have been widely and repeatedly read, fully qualifying them to be classics. At the same time, that such works appeared only in this period may serve as additional substantiation of my earlier observations, because it leads me to suspect that the eastern warriors of the Kamakura period had a distinctive society and that *ie* society's functioning in such a pure form was an exceptional, temporary phenomenon in Japanese history.

The Discovery of Skill and Taste

The interest in the private, personal world passed down from the Heian period gave rise, in the late Kamakura and early Muromachi periods, to a social climate of respect for individual skills and tastes. As Kyoto urbanized and its residents diversified, the values of the aristocracy gradually lost their sway, giving way to the ideals of people who worked with their hands—warriors, merchants, and artisans.

Kenkō's *Tsurezuregusa* is the most prominent example of the plentiful documentation of this change. The transitional nature of Kenkō's time is reflected in the contradictory positions he took in his observations on the distinctive abilities of individuals. On the one hand, he inherited the spirit of the Heian nobility, which made him somewhat suspicious of individual talent. Court nobles saw no particular value in uniqueness; on the contrary, they considered it a virtue to follow the ideals codified by tradition. Although having talent was, of course, not a bad thing, sweating away at polishing it was not considered becoming.

In some respects Kenkō perpetuated this aesthetic attitude, observing that it "is unbecoming and unseemly" for an elderly person to work sedulously to improve his accomplishments. On the other hand, he imbibed the atmosphere of the new age, commenting affirmatively on the diversity of human talent, which he saw from a broad perspective. *Tsurezuregusa* not only lauds ability in tanka and archery but also singles out experts in various crafts among the nameless common people, including a famous tree climber and proficient waterwheel makers, viewing with warm approval people whose lives are completely bound up in their skills.

Accompanying growing acclaim for such expertise was a pronounced improvement in the evaluation of individual preferences and tastes. In the Heian period the assertion of individual taste was not yet an active virtue and, as is evident in traditional painting, people were oriented toward stereotyping even facial features and expressions. Displaying the conflicting feelings born of a transitional age, Kenkō himself was a stubborn man of taste who at the same time

48

looked askance at people who made a show of their preferences and imported luxuries from the continent.

In the late fourteenth century, however, a rebellious aesthetic sense appeared, primarily in the warrior class. *Basara*,
for example, emerged as a new value that made a virtue of
a perverse, defiant attitude. In the *Taiheiki* a *basara* feudal
lord named Sasaki Dōyo (1306–73, also known as Sasaki
Takauji) is depicted as violating all sorts of social norms
but at the same time enjoying eye-catching displays in aesthetic pursuits, such as the tea ceremony and *renga*. What
is more, his ostentation overwhelms his political enemies
psychologically, winning him the acceptance of society at
large and elevating his social status. Not only Dōyo but all
influential warriors and wealthy figures of the day dis-
played their tastes in some sort of amusement, pouring their
energies into refined pursuits. It was fashionable to spend
huge sums on entertainments or on antique curios that took
one's fancy, such as the tea ceremony, music and dance,
or Chinese art objects.

Multilayered Self-expression

Eventually the expression of personal preference went beyond mere orientation toward luxury and ostentation, ma-
turing gradually into a lofty inner aesthetic. The leading
example is probably the tea ceremony. Its development was
begun by Murata Shukō (1422–1502), a Buddhist priest
who reputedly served as Yoshimasa's tea master at Ginkakuji. Shukō's emphasis on the spiritual aspects of the tea
ceremony was further developed by a Sakai tea master,

Takeno Jōō (1504–55), and his disciple, Sen no Rikyū (1522–91), who perfected the aesthetic of simple, austere serenity known as *wabi*. Through the tea ceremony people entertained others and enjoyed their company, at the same time developing the subtle interpersonal relations that marked this age of turmoil and strife. In a tumultous world where insubordination was rife and a person might be betrayed at any time, personal relationships took on special importance, and one's life depended on cultivating them carefully. Through tea gatherings people not only judged the political influence and financial power of their associates but also endeavored to ferret out delicate shades of character and capacity for finesse. Out of this grew extremely complex negotiations regarding self-expression and the paradoxical spirit of *wabi*, which strives to assert the self by suppressing the self.

The dual-image structure of *wabi* as an aesthetic principle is illustrated by the overlapping expression that is created when the splendor of a full moon is covered by a scrap of cloud or when the sumptuous Chinese style is enveloped in the simplicity of Japanese style. In the *Nanbōroku*, a collection of Rikyū's teachings on the tea ceremony compiled by one of his disciples, Jōō is said to have considered the spirit of *wabi* to be symbolized in a poem by Fujiwara no Teika (1162–1241):

As far as the eye can see,
No cherry blossoms,
No leaves in their autumn tints:
Only a thatched hut by a lagoon
This autumn evening.[6]

The important point here is that the courtly beauty of cherry blossoms and autumn foliage exists in the first place; true *wabi* comes into being when these can be imagined through the haze of autumn dusk.

In other words, at the root of an expressive statement lies the unreserved self-assertion of its originator, which when manifested paradoxically becomes a distinctive form of self-effacement. This was probably the most effective means of warding off the aversion that was apt to be incurred by direct self-assertion, as well as of preventing the other party from becoming bored. By exercising restraint, the person initiating the expression could disarm the other person, at the same time emphasizing inner grandeur through the dramatic contrast with overtly expressed simplicity and refinement.

This layered expression of the self is a major feature of Japanese literature from the Kamakura through the Edo period and can be inferred, for example, from Zeami's philosophy of "no action" in noh. "No action" was a plaudit that contemporary noh connoisseurs awarded outstanding actors who exercised restraint in displaying their virtuosity. Spectators with vivid imaginations saw greater artistry in this restraint than in overt dramatization. Considering this effect important, Zeami encouraged actors to adopt it as a strategy. In the early stage of an actor's development, this meant setting aside the audience's expectations and not revealing techniques that should be shown, but in its more advanced form it demanded that the actor hide his awareness of technique in general. In other words, the actor creating the expression had to conceal even from himself his intention to move others, his awareness of his own contrivance. Zeami taught that what is concealed will flower; what is not concealed will not flower.

The same structure can be found in the term *yūgen* as used in medieval poetry critiques, and it is also evident in the Edo period, attesting to the keen interest the Japanese have in self-expression. The entire tradition is informed by a desire to realize the self through aesthetic expression and to achieve this by taking care to differentiate self-expression from vainglory. That is, while fully expressing oneself, one tries to avoid having one's own self-expression intrude on other people's egos and to establish one's personal individuality within an aesthetic agreement with others. This approach has neither the arrogance of modern individualism, which constantly turns other people into a means of self-realization and therefore struggles with others, nor the indolence of groupism, which is a kind of collusion that is unconscious of others from the start. It is instead a gentle individualism that fears others even while placing them in close proximity and aims to realize the self within the context of other people's evaluation.[7]

I might add that in medieval Japan this sort of aesthetic expression was widely acclaimed and sometimes moved events with the same force as military might or financial power. Anecdotes abound of such incidents as a victorious general demanding aromatic wood instead of territory, a defeated military leader's life being spared because he handed over his tea ceremony equipment, or the lord of a castle being saved from defeat because he knew the secret interpretations of the ancient poetry contained in the *Kokinshū* anthology compilation (completed in 905) that teachers transmitted orally to their disciples. The majority of these tales may have little basis in fact, but that they have been handed down is evidence enough that this was part of the social ethos.

Artists and Impresarios

From this unique cultural milieu emerged a great number of dynamic impresario-type figures. They both created art and culture and served as cultural entrepreneurs who organized large numbers of creative people, acting as intermediaries in presenting their work to society. On the one hand these impresarios were rebels rejecting the vulgarity of the real world; on the other hand they were realists, capable of hobnobbing both with those at the height of power and with the masses. They embodied a dramatic spirit having a dual inner world.

The earliest forerunner of this type was probably Zeami, a powerful actor and writer as well as the leader of the Kanze school of noh. Possessed of an exceedingly lofty aesthetic sense, he was a lonely figure, conceited enough to boast that future audiences would be unable to understand the simple refinement of plays, such as *Kinuta*, that he had written. At the same time, he sought to gain the support of a broad spectrum of the public, striving to win the love and respect of the masses and also going to great lengths to obtain Shogun Ashikaga Yoshimitsu's patronage. The tense conflict between his artistic self-esteem and his concern that performances succeed as entertainment, between his assertion of self and his concern with society, caused him to give actors instructions that in some instances sound almost cynical, telling them to perform in a way that would be interesting even to spectators lacking the ability to judge a play.

This emotional conflict sensitized Zeami to relations between the self and others in a philosophical sense as well, making him keenly aware of the basic nature of the ego. According to Zeami, subjective awareness, or *gaken*, alone will not give an actor a complete picture of self. To truly liberate the self an actor must have control over the "rear view," which requires seeing the self through other people's eyes, or *riken*. Thus, achieving self-perfection requires a paradoxical effort to incorporate other people's gaze into one's own consciousness, in other words, to develop the ability to see oneself objectively.

As head of a troupe, Zeami organized people with varied skills—actors, musicians, and makers of masks and costumes. He also integrated elements from a number of different contemporary performing genres. He valued the diversity of talent assembled under his aegis and praised individuals by name, but at the same time he warned them against self-importance.

Living in close proximity to warrior society, Zeami believed in the concept of *ie*, but to him it bore no relation to consanguineous legitimacy or continuity achieved through heredity. *Ie* as he used the term meant purely the genealogy through which techniques possessed by individuals were handed down, in other words, the continuity of an artistic school. With regard to this he taught: "An art should not be passed on to an incompetent, even if he is your only son." This was a philosophy stressing competence: "An *ie* is not automatically an *ie* but becomes one by virtue of being passed on to a suitable successor; a person is not automatically a person but becomes one by virtue of knowledge." This made his idea of *ie* totally different from the warrior concept of lineage, which aimed for continuity of legitimacy based on the consanguineous inheritance of land. In fact, the Kanze school that Zeami led died out after he exiled himself to the island of Sado in his later years, his own aesthetics at odds with the tastes of Shoguns Ashikaga Yoshimochi and Yoshinori.

In the Momoyama period the tea master Sen no Rikyū fulfilled a role similar to Zeami's and met a similar fate. Rikyū, the scion of a Sakai merchant family, was originally a businessman who became tea master and aesthetic advisor to Toyotomi Hideyoshi, thus establishing *wabi* as the official taste of the day. While, on the one hand, he introduced this new aesthetic into the conservative court, there is also evidence that he fulfilled the role of Hideyoshi's advisor with respect to domestic political affairs as well.

The relationship between power holder and artist went beyond that of patronage and service. Hideyoshi and Rikyū were undoubtedly linked by a more complex interdependence regarding self-expression. By making Rikyū his "front man" Hideyoshi was able to control the entire nation, down to its deepest aesthetic attitudes; by taking on Hideyoshi's radiance Rikyū was able to enhance the spell his self-expression exerted over society. The aesthetic of *wabi* being a multilayered form of expression, the relationship between Hideyoshi and Rikyū can be considered the embodiment of this layering.

Rikyū, like Jōō before him, expressed the aesthetic of *wabi* in terms of the poem by Fujiwara no Teika cited earlier, but he also likened it to a thoroughbred horse tied up in a straw hut. He built a lavish, gilded teahouse for Hideyoshi and also outfitted a tiny teahouse fashioned like a mountain hut in one corner of Hideyoshi's great castle. It may not be stretching the point to take the view that to the inner Rikyū, Hideyoshi was the famous horse, the cherry blossoms and autumn leaves, while to Hideyoshi, Rikyū was the straw hut and the autumn dusk.

A relationship of this sort is fraught with tension, however, and it is not difficult to imagine that a slight shift in the perception of self could lead to jealousy and hatred. In his later years Rikyū intensified his confrontation with Hideyoshi, eventually receiving a death sentence for his "crimes." Numerous explanations of what specifically occasioned this confrontation have been offered, but a psychological conflict over self-expression is fully conceivable, at least hidden in the background. Noteworthy among the charges against Rikyū were that he created distinguished new tea utensils of his own in addition to those that already existed and that he had an image of himself made and placed on display in the gate of the temple Daitokuji. Rikyū's art lay basically in producing the tea ceremony as a form of socializing, acting as impresario to a group of artisans spanning many fields, from potters to carpenters. In his later years he strengthened his entrepreneurial side, and when he himself gradually began to play the part of a patron of the arts, his ego probably collided with Hideyoshi's.

Today the tea ceremony presents the model form of the *iemoto* system, wherein the head (*moto*) of an artistic school (*ie*) passes the art on to talented disciples. Rikyū, who brought the tea ceremony to perfection, was a lonely figure who lived his last days caught up in a struggle between two strong personalities that ended when, in full pride, he delivered himself the death blow.

Another important artistic figure, active slightly later than Rikyū, was Hon'ami Kōetsu (1558–1637). He was born into a prominent Kyoto family that repaired and appraised swords. He was a follower of the Nichiren sect of Buddhism, which is very strict about personal belief. This sect teaches the doctrine of salvation by one's own efforts and has features of strongly self-reliant individualism. It had many adherents among the merchants and artisans of Kyoto and may have underwritten their sense of honesty and good faith, just as Calvinism did in the West.

Kōetsu's mother was a bold defiant woman who had no fear of those in power. A family history records that once when a thief broke into the house and stole a customer's sword she declared that a wealthy warrior would not be inconvenienced by such a trifling loss and refused to make an issue of it. On the contrary, she took pity on the impoverished thief, sending money to the temple where she worshiped to have prayers offered for the culprit's safe escape. Kōetsu, heir to her ethical sense and rebellious spirit, detested the petty miserliness common among small merchants. A story has it that a friend told him that he paid all his bills at the year's end when everyone was busiest. When Kōetsu asked the reason, the friend replied that the confusion enabled him to shortchange the bill collectors. Enraged, Kōetsu broke off the relationship.

Kōetsu was typical of the impresario-artist. A brilliant calligrapher, potter, and designer of books and lacquerware in his own right, he organized a large number of highly talented friends working in many fields. Among them were the tea master Oda Urakusai, or Uraku, (1547–1621); the tea master Furuta Oribe (1544–1615); the potter Raku Jōkei, whose family began making Raku ware tea vessels for Rikyū and has continued in this occupation down to the present day; Nagoshi Sanshō, a forger of iron teakettles whose family would be renowned kettle makers for generations to come; and the laquer artist Igarashi Tahei, whose family was long influential in this field.

The conversations and joint projects that took place within this circle produced many valuable results. The most famous of these was *Sagabon*, illustrated texts of the Japanese classics, which Kōetsu published together with Suminokura Soan (1571–1632, also known as Yoshida Soan). These elegant masterpieces brought together the fruits of contemporary arts, including papermaking, illustrating, and bookbinding.

In his later years Kōetsu established an artists' village at Takagamine, in the hills of northern Kyoto, creating a community where such figures as the wealthy merchant Chaya Shirōjirō, the artist Ogata Sōhaku, and Fudeya Myōki, a maker of calligraphy brushes, shared the aesthetic life. Neither the *ie*-based extended kinship grouping of the warrior class nor an occupational grouping like those found among peasants and craftsmen, this group comprised individuals having different lineages and occupations who came together to share their devotion to the Nichiren sect and their personal tastes. In other words, it was a community that replicated the spirit of the city, a rarity in history and probably the world's first experiment in establishing an art colony.

Belief in Human Universality

Suminokura Soan, Kōetsu's partner in publishing the *Sagabon*, and his father, Ryōi (1554–1614), were the leading entrepreneurs of medieval Japan. The Suminokura family, moneylenders in the Saga district of Kyoto, stemmed from a long line of physicians. Soan's grandfather had traveled to Ming China as a doctor, returning with a great many medical books. His cosmopolitan interests and respect for technology requiring advanced knowledge seem to have had a definitive influence on Ryōi and Soan.

Ryōi, the legitimate heir of the Suminokura family, relinquished his position to his younger brother and embarked on new ventures as a free individual. The first of these was overseas trade centering on Annam, part of present-day Vietnam. The second was riparian engineering projects that opened a number of major rivers to navigation, which enabled him to go into the shipping business on these waterways. The latter were public-works projects having considerable relation to the national government and requiring advanced knowledge and technology. They were, moreover, highly dangerous and depended heavily on the individual's spirit of adventure. Ryōi took the initiative in investing in these ventures, managing laborers in many fields, ranging from seafaring to civil engineering, and invented new excavating technology. A posthumous statue of him was carved in accordance with his will, an act reminiscent of Rikyū. The keen-eyed, purposeful expression of the figure, excavating tools in hand, impressively sums up Ryōi's attitude toward life.

Soan continued all his father's projects, in particular developing Ryōi's scholastic and artistic interests. His publishing business was an especially outstanding success, but he also gave depth to his father's long-cherished desires regarding Confucianism, maintaining close relations with two great scholars of the day, Fujiwara Seika (1561–1619) and Hayashi Razan (1583–1657). Soan and Seika cooperated in foreign trade and worked out a philosophical theory to justify international commerce. Seika drew up ship's rules for the government-authorized trading ships operated by Soan and drafted letters to the king of Annam that express vividly the view of trade and the international perspective held by the Confucianists of medieval Japan. These documents emphasize *shin*, or good faith, using it to justify commercial activity and explain human universality.

Seika warned the Japanese traders on the ships against profiteering, arguing that because trade is a means of benefiting oneself and others by providing goods that are available in one place to another place that lacks them, coprosperity based on good faith will lead to greater profits than will cheating. The ship's oath that he drafted states explicitly:

Foreign lands may differ from our own in manners and speech, but as to the nature bestowed upon men by heaven there cannot be any difference. Do not forget the common identity and exploit differences. Beware even of minor lies and cheating, of arrogance and cursing. The foreigner may not be aware of them but you certainly will be. "Good faith reaches to the pig and fish, and trickery is seen by the seagulls." Heaven does not tolerate deception. Be mindful, therefore, not to bring disgrace upon our country's tradition. In case you meet men of benevolence and education, respect them as you would your own father or teacher. Inquire into the restrictions and taboos of the country, and act in accordance with its customs and religion.[8]

To the Annamese king, who despised trade and attached overwhelming importance to Confucian principles, he reasoned that poetry and good manners were means of ruling the country well, asserting that trade undertaken in good faith could make an important contribution to the same end. In a letter to the king, Seika wrote:

Your letter says that the only thing important is the word "good faith"; it is the essence of morality in the nation and the home. We too hold to the belief that good faith is inherent in our nature, that it moves heaven and earth, penetrates metals and rocks, and pervades everything without exception; its influence is not just limited to contact and communication between neighboring countries. The winds may blow in different directions in countries a thousand miles apart, but as to good faith every quarter of the world must be the same, for this is the very nature of things.

It will be seen therefore that men differ only in secondary details, such as clothing and speech. Countries may be a thousand or even ten thousand miles apart and differences may be found in clothing and speech, but there is one thing in all countries which is not far apart, not a bit different: that is good faith.[9]

In other words, he postulated "good faith" as a shared international ethic and the principle underlying commerce. Thus, if people acted in good faith, they would be able to overcome cultural disparities and join in ties of friendship while accepting differences of custom.

In addition to being tolerant of other cultures, Seika proposed universal principles of international exchange. He interpreted Confucianism, the philosophical lingua franca of the day, in his own way, emphasizing the principle of good faith in particular and advocating it to the rest of the world from the Japanese standpoint. The position evidenced here was realistic, reducing poetry and propriety to good government and affirming mercantile activity as a means to the same end, as well as universalistic and individualistic, seeing human beings as essentially the same regardless of ethnic or national identity. That the Japanese once espoused this sort of philosophy is in itself interesting, but even more impressive is the fact that they stated it in cosmopolitan terms and endeavored to make it the common foundation for international negotiation. Although these early international traders saw that Japanese culture was different, they did not consider it unique, and the public realm in which they had faith domestically crossed the seas unchanged, serving as an avenue of intercultural communication.

Managers of the Culture Industry

Once the Edo period had reached its height the Japanese undeniably cut a less imposing figure than had these Renaissance-type personalities. The Tokugawa shogunate's seclusionist policy isolated Japanese society from the international environment, and its physiocratic ethos placed restraints on urban commercial and cultural activities. Closing the country obviously reduced opportunities for foreign trade and investment, and stratifying society into warrior, peasant, artisan, and merchant classes limited merchants' social position, restricting their participation in public-works projects involving the government. Edo-period townsmen forged ties with feudal lords throughout the country, and some merchants, such as Yamagata Bantō (1748–1821), were even hired to apply their business skills to improving fief finances, but lending money to feudal lords also placed merchants in danger of bankruptcy.

Under these circumstances many merchants, such as those of the Mitsui family, protected themselves by creating a conservative *ie* organization. Others experienced drastic ups and downs, amassing fortunes through investment and squandering them in a generation. Obviously, neither pattern was apt to breed giants like Ryōi and Soan, but the shogunate's suppression of urban culture itself went even further toward stifling merchant initiative. Under the pretext of prohibiting luxury, the government placed theater, literature, and art under strict surveillance and frequently devised excuses for punishing unlucky patrons of the arts.

Despite this, however, the townspeople had tremendous enthusiasm for culture, and the line of impresario-artists and entrepreneurial culture makers continued. In fact, as time passed culture became increasingly mass oriented; the arts spread among the masses as pastimes, in response to which entrepreneurs who produced popular culture came to the fore. Their work included theater management, art dealing, publishing, and private-school management and even extended into certain areas of the distribution industry, such as the kimono trade. All these occupations demanded creativity and a spirit of adventure, as well as the ability to understand the masses so as to win their love and respect. These were uncertain ventures that dealt in information more than goods, drew their customers from the multitudes, and always involved risk, but any number of townsmen had the daring to take up such challenges and succeed.

One such was the publisher Tsutaya Jūzaburō (1750–97), a self-made man who started out by retailing a guide to the pleasure quarters. Eventually he began publishing the guide himself, rising rapidly to dominate the publishing industry. Publishing was a model "culture industry," partly because it demanded a feeling for trends and foresight but also because it early established the concept of honesty in business. Jūzaburō's rise to success began when another publisher was punished for plagiarism by having his property confiscated and being banished. Strict ethical regulations like this may have kept business competition for new ideas clean.

Jūzaburō expanded the range of his publications: *kibyōshi*, satirizing the life of the times; *sharebon*, novelettes based on life in the pleasure quarters; textbooks; and *kyōkashū*, farcical poetry collections parodying the traditional tanka. Eventually he became a leading publisher of *ukiyoe* woodblock prints. His weapons in all these endeavors were the insight to discern talent and a knack for socializing that enabled him to organize people with distinctive personalities. Jūzaburō patronized and fraternized with a long list of figures who collectively constituted the essence of Edo culture: the novelist and poet Hōseido Kisanji; the author and illustrator Koikawa Harumachi; the poet and fiction writer Ōta Nanpo; the *ukiyoe* artist Kitagawa Utamaro; the writer and artist Santō Kyōden, whose artworks bear the name Kitao Masanobu; the critic, diarist, novelist, and poet Takizawa Bakin; and the *ukiyoe* artist Tōshūsai Sharaku.

Socializing tended to take place in Yoshiwara and other pleasure quarters. Jūzaburō joined in the popular *kyōka* parties, taking great pains to understand these artists, who had many quirks. In spirit these gatherings had much in common with the earlier salons of Rikyū, Kōetsu, and Soan, although the passage of time had made them the property of the common people. The salons of the Edo period were wide open to the public, and their products enjoyed a popularity that would be amazing even today, such as an illustrated novel that sold well over 10,000 copies.

Needless to say, as an industry publishing is not an enormous presence, and even if the entire gamut of culture industries were included, they would not leave much of a mark on economic history. But the entrepreneurial spirit that underwrote them may have made a significant if unseen contribution to modern Japan's industrialization. At the least, it must be borne in mind that premodern Japan had a group of entrepreneurs of this type and that the social milieu allowing them to exist had a 300-year history. In addition to industriousness, loyalty, homogeneity, and a spirit of cooperation—the core characteristics of so-called Japanese-style management—another traditional ethos was constantly present.

According to Tanaka Yūko, an authority on Edo literature, the personal relations supporting this free ethos were
symbolized by *ren*, salons for creating haiku and *kyōka*,
literary genres that Jūzaburō loved. The verses were composed, admired, and evaluated at social gatherings, becoming the central bond in the salons, in emulation of the
tradition that had existed since *renga*, linked verse, came
into being. Sometimes a *ren* was based on community ties,
and occasionally it took the form of a nationwide network
linking meeting places and relay points. A *ren*, formed for
the sole purpose of creating poetry, was a loose organization that had no relation to status or occupation, philosophy
or religious belief. In the eighteenth century *ren* spread
throughout Japanese society, with large numbers of commoners joining in the pleasure of creating poetry.

Tanaka sees the *ren* style of association as the social foundation of much of Edo-period culture. In her view, the scholars who assembled around the physician Sugita Genpaku
(1733–1817) to translate the few Dutch scientific works
available and the network for the study of herbs established
by the naturalist Hiraga Gennai (1726–79) constituted types
of *ren*. Gennai organized a nationwide network of collection agencies and middlemen to provide himself with a
route for gathering herb samples for exhibition. Tanaka tells
us that he got this idea from the haiku *ren*. Whether or not
a direct connection between the two exists, both involved
a similar sense of interpersonal relations.

The important point here is that in the Edo period information and goods were frequently distributed through net-
works based on free personal relationships and that the

populace had faith in and respect for such relationships. All this undoubtedly contributed significantly to the formation of a capitalist free market when Japan underwent industrialization.

Chapter Four:
Ie Society and Contextual Theory

Tᴴɪꜱ tradition of individualism notwithstanding, Japan has never been a ruggedly individualistic society of the sort found in the West, and after it began modernizing diametrically opposed features became prominent.

As the Japanese have intensified their contacts with the West over the past century, they have acquired a reputation both at home and abroad for being reticent as individuals and masters of attentiveness within an organization but inept at social interaction across organizational lines. For 1,400 years the Japanese have been taught that living in harmony is a virtue, and they have long been fond of repeating the medieval maxim that a bundle of three arrows is stronger than each arrow alone. In the workplace people still make half-jesting remarks about the importance of the company organization and the priority of the job. To be sure, the joking tone contains subtle nuances that point more to the Japanese ability to put up a good front than to a serious sense of loyalty, but superficially, at least, such comments are the unmistakable mark of a group orientation. And a familistic ethos not found in other countries is prominent in the organizational structure, management, and operation of the corporations and government agencies that are at the core of modern Japanese society.

Strongly individualistic, dictatorial business leaders, such as America's Lee Iacocca, are a rarity, particularly in prominent companies that have passed through several generations since their founding. In Japan such individualistic chief executives are generally found in venture businesses and relatively new industrial fields, occasionally even in fairly sizable firms. But the majority of large corporations uphold the principle of achieving consensus through *ringi*, that is, obtaining sanction for a proposal by circulating a draft for all concerned to sign, and *nemawashi*, behind-the-scenes negotiation. Middle-level managers essentially run the organization, and mechanisms exist for conveying their views to the top smoothly. Although a meeting may start with many differences of opinion, a conclusion is rarely reached by one side predominating over the other. Even the principle of majority rule tends to be avoided as much as possible. Instead, the majority tenaciously applies persuasion, and the meeting generally winds up with the minority magnanimously acquiescing. By Western standards, the individual members of the organization are flexible in their assertions and demands, and the way they transmit their views does not seem to be logical or conceptual. The members are already joined by tacit understandings and in the meeting are merely making minor adjustments. This is frequently considered to be the traditional mode of communication among the Japanese.

Over the past century, this orientation toward harmonization has at times overstepped reasonable limits and taken the form of totalitarianism, that is, domination by the group. Frequently the nation, family, and bureaucratic organization have suppressed the individual, and the person standing at the apex of the system has appeared to be an arrant dictator.

The Discovery of a New Familism

Many modern intellectuals, particularly writers, have been bewitched by this phenomenon, perceiving Japanese society as one of feudalistic lineage and stronghanded patriarchal domination. Not only those who have denounced the system from a Marxist perspective but also intellectuals of a liberal bent, who constitute the great majority, have looked on the national government and corporations with extreme suspicion. Writers, in particular, have seen themselves as oppressed by "the village," grounded in ties of locale, and the *ie*, based on consanguineous ties, within which the symbolic enemy has always been the father. In early modern Japanese literature, the father symbolized Japan's suppressive ethos, and escaping from paternal restraints meant freedom for the individual. Writers, unaware that this suppression was a product of distortions caused by modernization, impetuously projected the present situation onto the past, generally seeing the former as a remnant of feudalism.

After World War II, however, the groups constituting Japanese society lost much of their capacity to be suppressive, and certain rights and freedoms were guaranteed to individuals, finally enabling perceptive intellectuals to discern the essential nature of Japanese groups.

Such intellectuals have come to realize that although these groups are familistic, grounded in cooperation and tacit understanding, they are neither totalitarian organizations with ironclad rules nor communities to which a person is fated to belong by virtue of birth in a given locale or family. This is the achievement of Murakami, Kumon, and Satō in *Bunmei to shite no ie shakai* and the contribution of the sociologist Hamaguchi Eshun, who has given the name "contextual" to this type of interpersonal relationship. This new perspective is, of course, the fruit of the imaginations of the people who formulated the concepts, but it can also be considered to be the result of changes in social realities that have freed the past from projections of realities now outdated.

⌈Since this study reconsiders the traditions of Japanese society in an effort to define Japan's distinctive form of individualism, it may be addressing, from the opposite direction, the same question as the *ie* theory, which, motivated by the same considerations, has revealed the salient features of the Japanese people's group orientation. As I have already suggested, *ie* society and gentle individualism are in reality two sides of the same coin. Sometimes they have been equally balanced; sometimes one or the other has predominated. But in either case, they have created the characteristics of Japanese culture and shaped Japanese history, at least since the medieval period. ⌋

At the end of the 1960s, when *Bunmei to shite no ie shakai* was written, Japanese society was overwhelmingly dominated by the *ie* principle, and other factors were almost completely invisible. It was not until nearly 20 years later that signs of gentle individualism first became evident. Until then Japanese society was, in fact, in a state that could be explained almost completely in terms of *ie* theory. The reasons for this will be examined later, but first a detailed introduction of this *ie* theory is in order.

According to *Bunmei to shite no ie shakai*, the *ie* is not a natural family joined by consanguineous ties or a lineage constituting a valid genealogy. The *ie* is not governed by simple authoritarian patriarchalism; biological lineage is not the principle holding it together.

The basis for the aforementioned scholars' assertions is Francis L. K. Hsu's theory of Japanese society and the concept of "kin-tract" that he originated. Hsu closely observed the relationship in Japan that is called the *ie*, comparing it with the concepts of family in China, India, and Europe. He found the Japanese *ie* to be one of the few family systems in the world employing formal adoption to continue the *ie* line when, for example, there are no consanguineous descendants. In most countries, the family is an organization of ties of blood, and inheritance by a scion is indispensable to continuation of the lineage. If an heir is not to be found, the family line dies out. In Japan, however, an effort is made to protect the form of the *ie* and perpetuate its nominal framework even if it means bringing in an outsider. This led Hsu to consider the Japanese *ie* to be a lineage as a formalized system rather than as a genealogical reality.

Even in modern times Japanese society has shown a propensity for adoptive relationships. Many Osaka merchants, for example, have handed over their *ie* to an adopted son even though they had natural sons. The product of a typically merchant realism, this practice has made it possible both to perpetuate the lineage and to utilize capable people by passing over a mediocre eldest child and adopting a talented employee married to a daughter. Even social groups that involve no blood relationships whatsoever are called *ikka* (literally, one *ie*), and the constituent members are referred to as *oyabun* (parent role) and *kobun* (child role). This likening of systematized organizations to the family is a prominent feature of Japanese society.

The Ambivalent *Ie*

Agreements with other people are inherent in such an *ie*, which is underwritten by the concept of contract. Needless to say, the family is normally held together by blood ties and lacks any concept of a public contract; apart from the marriage relationship, no conscious agreements are made. But with the Japanese *ie*, potentially at least, a public agreement comes into play at the most crucial juncture, when the estate is inherited. At the same time, because this fictive family is modeled on the consanguineous family, it necessarily resembles in character the consanguineous family. Once a person has been adopted into the *ie* by means of contractual agreement, the contract is transcended and the adopted person becomes a component member of the family household unconditionally, belonging to the *ie* forever. Hsu closely observed this dual character of the *ie*, calling it a "corporation" and the principle underlying it a "kin-tract," a neologism derived, obviously, from the words "kin" and "contract."

74

On the basis of Hsu's theory, Murakami, Kumon, and Satō undertook an in-depth, theoretical explanation of Japan's social structure, carefully supporting it with historical evidence. According to them, the Japanese *ie* is not a consanguineous family; what is more, it is not a grouping based on ties of locale, that is, a relationship developed in the village, where people are tied to the land. They maintain that the *ie* is first and foremost a business entity having a given purpose and therefore is a rationally functional grouping.

The prototype of the *ie* was created by the pioneering territorial lords who developed the Kantō plain of eastern Japan from the end of the Heian through the early Kamakura period. These rising lords developed virgin territory, expanded it, and created strong armed groups to defend it from enemies. The necessities of the harsh frontier environment forced warrior families to grow rapidly, and in the process they had to take in and organize a great many nonconsanguineous members.

The more artificial an organization, the greater the need to give it a theoretical raison d'être, but in the Kantō region during the pioneering period adopting abstract principles, such as religion, was difficult. For peasants and low-ranking warriors, many of whom were illiterate, a tangible, naturalistic principle was more effective, and consanguinity was probably the principle closest to hand. Comparing the relationship between lord and vassal to that between parent and child and assuring the lord's authority by means of inheritance was doubtlessly a principle of order that was easily comprehensible to anyone with a family. The wider the extent of violent struggles for supremacy outside the group, the greater the need within the group for an order that was not swayed by the vicissitudes of relative strength. The image of the natural family must have provided the most suitable tie on which to base internal order. Thus in Kanto warriors' groups relatives reinforced their cohesiveness as "children of the *ie*," and unrelated retainers, referred to as "people of the *ie*," acted as if they were family members.

Even toward the end of the medieval period, when warriors began leaving their designated territories and moving from place to place, this fictive family remained intact. The *ie* thus contrived to maintain and strengthen itself, striving to continue being a functional, effective fighting organization.

At the same time, because its objective was self-perpetuation, the time never came when the goals of the *ie* were attained and its function came to an end, so it came to resemble a living organism that unconditionally maintains itself forever. New followers whose abilities were favorably evaluated were admitted through a contract, but once they had joined the *ie*, they were considered to belong to it in perpetuity, down the generations.

In short, the *ie* is a natural group created artificially, a purpose-oriented association whose purpose cannot be clearly defined. To borrow a term from the sociologist Ferdinand Tönnies, it is essentially a *Gesellschaft*-like *Gemeinschaft*. This ambivalent organization with two contradictory aspects has resulted in a distinctive structure, which in turn has imparted special features to the way in which the *ie* functions.

First, because the *ie* is patterned on the consanguineous family, it must center on a consistent, continuous lineage. This can be called the "stem family," the central lineage that must form an unbroken, legitimate genealogy, whether through adopted or natural heirs. The stem family does not necessarily have actual power as group leader; on the contrary, it is generally regarded simply as the symbol of *ie* continuity and integrity. This central lineage must, however, be highly enough revered that it dominates collateral members; moreover, its perpetuation must be guaranteed by some sort of authority other than actual ability. The stem family maintains the naturalness of inheritance by legitimate, consanguineous heirs and is a condensation of the objectivelessness that constitutes one aspect of the *ie*.

As a business organization with a purpose, however, the *ie* must be operated through a functional chain of command. Murakami and his associates call this the functional hierarchy of the *ie*. In many cases, the central figure in this order is not from the lineage of the symbolic stem family. This hierarchy and genealogy reflect the heterogeneity and homogeneity within the group, respectively, and making both tenable enables each to supplement and adjust the other. In the *ie*, unlike a purpose-oriented business organization that is simply a profit-making group, the functional hierarchy is ameliorated by a familistic atmosphere. The authority of the genealogy also causes the constituent members to submit of their own volition, softening their self-assertion. This has resulted in a philosophy of consensus, similar to the *ringi* system and *nemawashi*, taking root within the *ie*.

The Validity and Limitations of *Ie* Theory

By now it should be clear that *ie* theory offers a convincing model for the structure that is adopted when the Japanese create a stable organization.

Beginning in the Kamakura period, organizations in every stratum of the warrior class—first and foremost the *ie* of successive shoguns and feudal lords—consistently took the form of a supraconsanguineous family. Frequently the genealogy and the functional hierarchy were handled by different entities: Under a symbolic shogun, power was actually wielded by regents, governors general, or senior statesmen. The highest ideal, even among the general run of warriors, was to continue the fictive family forever, and its perpetuation was frequently given priority over the life and reputation of its ruling figure as an individual. Countless tales relate how an *ie*-centered fictive kin group that had lost a battle or political struggle redeemed the *ie*'s inheritance rights by the death of the *ie* head, or how the retainers of an *ie* whose head had been killed fought to restore the *ie* rather than to avenge the head's name. According to Murakami and his associates, the imperial line, Japan's greatest lineage, is a remnant of ancient clan society, but it survived the upheaval of the medieval period thanks to the moral sense of *ie* society. Doubtless, this eventually contributed to the creation of the tradition whereby the entire Japanese nation is likened to a supraconsanguineous family with a political form that separates the symbol of authority from the real locus of power.

I fully concur with these scholars' contention that this *ie* structure eventually spread beyond the warrior class, influencing the formation of large merchant houses, of which Mitsui is a typical example. We are told that in such merchant *ie*, roles were divided among the eldest son, who inherited the estate, the person who acted in the parent role and executed the *ie* rules, and the person with jurisdiction over the *ie* business, the last of whom was chosen from among themselves by the *ie* members who had a share in the property.

Above all, the theory constructed by Murakami and his associates is cogent because it transcends history to explain modern Japanese society, in particular providing a successful interpretation of the behavior patterns of large corporations and bureaucratic organizations. This is a historic contribution to the theory of Japanese modernization in that it gives cohesive significance to Japanese social characteristics, differentiates them from both Western totalitarianism and feudal patriarchalism, and explains them in terms of their ready adaptability to modern industry.

Every theory has weaknesses, however, and the problem here is the authors' excessive concentration on the stable organization known as the *ie*; in other words, their view is restricted to stable behavior on the part of the people living within the *ie*. To be sure, in their overview of Japanese history Murakami and his associates have not overlooked the process by which temporary organizations, such as *tō* (political party) or *ikki* (gang), are created and eventually absorbed into the *ie*. By "stable," however, I do not mean that an organization is maintained in peace and quiet, but that even if it passes through violent upheaval its objectives and goals are immovable, rendering the organization stable with respect to its mission as a means of attaining them.

79

In other words, the objectives of the action taken by the members of the *ie* are stable, and their reasons for needing the organization do not change significantly.

The *ie* as defined by Murakami and his associates is indeed a model group for stable action, being based on the agricultural management practiced by the pioneering Kantō territorial lords and having an armed military group as its prototype. In this respect, temporary organizations like *tō* and *ikki* are essentially the same as the *ie*, making their absorption into the organizationally more stable *ie* only natural.

The motto of these early armed groups, and a phrase that has since come into popular use, was *issho kenmei*, which expresses determination to stake one's life on a piece of land, on defending and enlarging it—the unswerving goal of warriors with peasants' hearts. As long as people's livelihoods are based on control of land and sustained by harvests, their attitudes toward life are necessarily fixed. People engaged in farming are always presented with clear goals and means for attaining them. Agriculture involves growth but not bold leaps, sustained planning but never sudden gambles. Expanding the operation does not demand day-to-day choices and decisions but the accumulation of assiduous efforts in small matters. Moreover, the most effective way of working is as a group within which there is a division of labor. Because the land is eternal, perpetuating the group is imperative. Peasant life has never been amenable to recombining groups to accord with changes of purpose, or to an individual's moving from group to group.

Military groups are essentially conservative, their major concern being stability in both behavior and organizational structure. Individual battles demand measures adapted to circumstances, but the essence of battle lies in physically overcoming an enemy, an objective whose limits are fixed by the fitness of the fighting force and the quality of its weapons. Because it takes time to train troops and improved weapons are developed only sporadically, basic battle forms and military organizational structures tend to remain unchanged for long periods. Superficially, fighting groups appear to be driven by the commander's charisma, philosophy, or beliefs, but in fact they are sustained by customary behavior cultivated through daily training. In essence, fighting groups possess features typical of peasant society: Fortitude and the ability to cooperate are virtues that are generally rewarded by familistic care and a feeling of participation.

Obviously, when the essentially similar behavior patterns associated with agriculture and warfare overlap, they reinforce each other, creating a distinctive organization. *Ie* society is not the strange product of Japan's natural environment and mythological memory; it is clearly nothing more than a construct deriving from one pattern of human behavior. This being the case, it is logically possible that in any age people could have adopted a different behavior pattern, consequently creating a society differing from *ie* society. In fact, from the Muromachi period on, merchants living in the cities had a completely different way of life from the peasantlike warriors. The basis of the merchants' livelihood was not a parcel of land to be defended to the death but business opportunities and flows of capital and information. The need to seize opportunity and make the most of information obliged them to select goals and devise methods for accomplishing them moment by moment. Ongoing endeavor is, of course, necessary in commerce, too, but the resourcefulness to adapt to changing circumstances is equally indispensable, and the courage to accept risk and adventure is frequently called for.

In fact, the prominent merchants of the early Edo period changed their lines of work any number of times in the course of building up their houses, altering their attitudes to life accordingly. Suminokura was typical: A family that had long been physicians at one point held the post of head of the Kyoto *obi* makers' guild and was involved in manufacturing and wholesaling *obi*, of which it had no previous experience. Around the same time this family achieved success in money lending and used this as a springboard to expand rapidly into construction, transport, overseas trade, and publishing. These steps all demanded strong leadership on the part of the individual heading the family, and the turning points were marked by the names of Suminokura Munetada, Ryōi, and Soan.

For these merchants, continuity of the lineage never became a goal in its own right; this never had greater importance than the success of the business being conducted at any given time. Neither Hon'ami Kōetsu nor Suminokura Ryōi succeeded to the family estate, but both were allowed to make great use of family resources to achieve their personal ambitions. For them the original, consanguineous family was, of course, a focus of affection, but it did not necessarily become the main agent of their business ventures. Commerce, unlike agriculture, has a short enough turnover period between investment and profit to enable the completion of a cycle within an individual's lifetime. In commerce, only capital and the name of the business can be inherited across generations, and from the Muromachi through the Edo period both could easily be wiped out by one mistaken investment. Group consultation and a sense of participation seem to have played a minimal role in the hazardous decisions that were involved.

Although some Edo-period merchants' houses, such as Mitsui, passed the business on for many generations, the great majority of merchant families disappeared before there was time to inherit capital. According to Moriya Takeshi, a historian of Japanese entertainment, in the Genroku era there was a saying, "Only one generation for the rich guys"; the rapid rise and fall of merchant houses was taken for granted.

For one thing, business at the time had strong elements of gambling, and investments gravitated toward speculation in the commodities market or in loans to feudal lords. Of equal importance, however, was an urbanite orientation toward socializing and cultural refinements that entailed lavish consumption and thus depleted assets. Even as the merchants adhered to a traditional ethic of hard work and honesty, they possessed an aesthetic sense that numbered the acquisition of artistic and scholarly accomplishments among the qualifications of a gentleman. In Ihara Saikaku's *Kōshoku nidai otoko* (The life of the son of an amorous man) townspeople are ranked as *kanemochi*, (nouveaux riches), *bugensha* (solid citizens), and *yoi shu* (gentlemen), depending on their aesthetics. *Kanemochi* were despised by fellow merchants for their lack of taste and cultural attainments. The situation was probably similar to that among the Muromachi warriors. In Japan, whenever people's reliability is being put to the test in a highly competitive arena, the capacity for self-expression, including artistic taste, becomes a crucial factor. Taste and refinement in socializing ranked with good faith in importance to interpersonal relations among merchants, and both were manifested in the spirit of *ichigo ichie*, which means that every occasion for getting together has a once-in-a-lifetime significance, so that utmost attention should be devoted to making it perfect.

Under these circumstances, townspeople of the late seventeenth century vied to have their heirs acquire refined attainments, which frequently resulted in the second generation's coming to ruin and bringing about the downfall of the *ie*. In his *Chōnin kōkenroku* Mitsui Takafusa, the fourth head of the Mitsui *ie*, warned against having young people learn artistic accomplishments, arguing that they should work hard while young and dabble in the arts after reaching middle age. Such house rules enabled Mitsui to perpetuate the *ie* lineage, but it is also conceivable that the rules were necessitated by the treacherous social climate of the day. I might add that in Japan during this time the teaching of artistic accomplishments became a common occupation and the publication of lesson books was widespread.

Moriya also states that the seventeenth century saw the small monogamous family take form in the rural community, contributing to improved agricultural productivity. Probably concomitantly, the small merchant family, with parents and children as its nucleus, was also established in the cities. Becoming a solid citizen meant that a family used its own wits and ingenuity to go into business. This concept of family took hold during the Genroku era, paradoxically paralleled by growing mass patronization of the pleasure quarters. Even as they fostered the concept of familial love, the townspeople formed concepts of romance outside the family. For townspeople, the family may have been merely an entity created by individual wit and resourcefulness that could also be easily destroyed by an individual's emotions.

This view considerably limits the applicability of the concept of the *ie* defined as a fictive family; in terms of its significance at least, the *ie* thus defined can account for only half the principles governing Japanese social composition. A further problem is that observation of the *ie* takes as its starting point the custom of adoption, so that the explanation of the *ie*'s features begins with the means by which an individual gains secondary membership. In other words, the *ie* is analyzed entirely from the standpoint of continuity, with no attention to the circumstances under which an enterprise is undertaken and a new *ie* established. Every *ie* begins with the founder of a consanguineous family, through whose individual abilities the group is enlarged, but the behavior patterns of these individuals have been left out of the picture.

This leads me to suspect that the *ie*, even as a peasant or warrior organization, was a structure that appeared only in the second generation or later. The Kamakura shogunate is an example of a model *ie*, but as an entity the Hōjō clan, which supplied shogunal regents, came into being in the generation after the founder of the shogunate, Minamoto Yoritomo (1147–99). Strictly speaking, it was Hōjō Masako (1157–1225), Yoritomo's widow, who transformed the consanguineous overlordship of the Minamoto family into a management organization of the fictive family type, establishing government by regents, after which the shogunate can be explained entirely in terms of *ie* theory. But Masako, the figure who accomplished this great feat, demonstrated an intense individuality rare in Japanese history, remorselessly murdering her own father and son to achieve her ends.

The Tokugawa shogunate was also an *ie*, but its founder, Tokugawa Ieyasu (1542–1616), actually destroyed one *ie* and remade it from the outside. He started out by leading the hereditary vassals of the Matsudaira family, taking upon himself both the genealogy and the hierarchy of that *ie* as he fought. But once in control of the entire nation, he gradually set aside his faithful followers of the battlefield, employing new, bureaucratic subordinates to build up the shogunate organization for the purpose of ruling the nation. Moreover, Ieyasu himself did not belong to this new *ie* organization; instead he withdrew to the status of retired shogun, a ploy that enabled him to maintain his dictatorial powers.

From the time of the first pioneering territorial lords, a great many *ie* rose and fell in a perpetual cycle of establishment and reorganization, and individualistic heroes similar to these must have appeared each time. Moreover, most of these heroes, such as the warlords Oda Nobunaga and Toyotomi Hideyoshi, flouted the *ie* principle; they believed in themselves and their blood relatives, but there is no evidence that they trusted in anything like a "kin-tract." I dare say that Japanese society's having given rise to a great number of *ie* means that there have also been an equal number of anti-*ie* individualists.

Moreover, even loyal members of *ie* society frequently had strong ties to other types of relationships while retaining their *ie* membership. Of great significance in this respect were the relationships between a teacher and his disciples, as well as the *ren* and other types of social salons. Talented samurai from domains across the country flocked to the schools of Edo, where emotional bonds developed that sometimes influenced these people's actions more strongly than ties with the domain. Toward the end of the Edo period, in particular, many learned samurai were hired by the lords of other domains or by the shogunate and, receiving official permission to belong to both organizations at once, devoted themselves to writing or teaching. Among them were the scholar Sakuma Shōzan (1811–64), who left the Matsushiro domain, in what is now Nagano prefecture, to work for the shogunate and the philosopher-politician Yokoi Shōnan (1809–69), a native of the Kumamoto domain who served in the Fukui domain and, together with his feudal lord, acted as an advisor on reforming the shogunate.

Japanese society values information, but historically, the relationships through which information was transmitted generally existed outside the *ie* framework. This tendency was especially pronounced in times of social change, when groups of individuals linked by information boldly took action in a milieu divorced from the organization of primary affiliation. A case in point is the Meiji Restoration of 1868. The politically peaceful fashion in which this tremendous reform was accomplished may be explicable in terms of this phenomenon. The need for Japan to modernize was heralded by far-sighted pioneers like Shōzan and Shōnan and, on an individual basis, was fairly well understood by loyalists and reformers alike. The reformers took action across

87

domain borders because their loyalty to information took precedence over their loyalty to the feudal organization; the same can be said of the more knowledgeable of the shogun's retainers. When the shogunate was dismantled, only a small minority died to defend the *ie*. The active contribution the loyalist elite later made to the formation of the Meiji government has many implications.

The Pros and Cons of Contextualist Theory

Like *ie* theory, the concept termed contextualism, used to substantiate the existence of the *ie*, has both strengths and weaknesses as an interpretation of history and as a critique of civilization. In particular, whereas *ie* is strictly a sociological concept, contextualism has more philosophical implications, which may impart greater weight to its significance as a vehicle for evaluating civilizations. Chapter Seven will examine contextualism in detail, but a brief discussion of its pros and cons, as well as the questions it raises, is in order here.

Contextualism was conceived as a concept critical of and juxtaposed upon the concept of the modern Western individual. According to its originator, Hamaguchi Eshun, the two are antithetical on three counts. As opposed to the individual, which originated in the West and is characterized by self-centeredness, self-reliance, and the view of interpersonal relations as a means, the Japanese contextual is distinguished by interdependence, mutual trust, and the view of interpersonal relations as intrinsically valuable. The Western individual considers the self to be the central rationale for forming society, believes that the power to fulfill human desires lies within the self, and regards relations with other people as a means to this end. The contextual considers relations of assistance and cooperation with other people to be the essential nature of life, acts on the premise of mutual tacit surmise, and makes interpersonal relations an objective in their own right, living in the unconditional hope that they will last forever.

To be specific, the contextual appears in the form of small groups that have their own characteristics and experiences and operate as distinctive units. The contextual is conceptualized as a fundamental unit of society that operates in the same dimension as the individual, granting it the qualifications of an actor, an implementer of human behavior. In contrast to the individual, which is a solid unit that cannot be subdivided, the contextual is a flexible unit that maintains a certain degree of unity within a context. It operates like a clause in a sentence, having a level of cohesiveness intermediate between that of the individual word and that of the sentence as a whole and mediating between the two. Just as the true meaning of a sentence appears in the clause, true social individuality appears within the contextual, which gives character both to the individual and to the group as a whole.

The contextual is neither the simple sum total of individuals nor a fragment of the whole; like the atoms that combine to form a molecule, it can become an actor having unique properties. While it comprises a number of different people, the contextual makes decisions and choices in the same way as a single ego and can also cooperate or compete with other contextuals.

Obviously, contextual theory was designed to criticize Western individualism, which has often been considered absolute, and to refute those Westerners who have denounced the group centeredness of Japanese society. Contextualism is valuable in that it probes the way existing arguments have posed their questions rather than simply making an issue of popular misunderstandings or weighing the good and bad points of different cultures.

Up to now sociology has juxtaposed the concepts of the individual and the totality, questioning which is true existence or which is theoretically first; contextual theory, however, negates the opposition of these two categories by setting up an intermediary category called the contextual. Society is definitely neither the overall harmonization of isolated particles called individuals nor the organic ethnic whole that romanticists have likened to "blood" or "soil." First there is a relationship with a specific neighbor whose face is known, and the individual can discover his or her individuality through interaction with this neighbor; society as a whole is a chain of tiny relationships of this sort. To put it in philosophical terms, the substance does not exist first and create relationships; relationships exist first and create the substance. In this respect contextual theory has had a Copernican effect in overthrowing ingrained concepts.

This line of thought enables us to take a view of society that is closer to reality and to answer plausibly the question of why both the individual and the whole can change while maintaining their identities at least to some degree. Contextual theory also makes it possible for humanity to avoid the tragic antinomy of dreadful disorder caused by individual self-assertion versus loss of freedom through totalitarian control. Most of all, it allows the Japanese to make a case for their own nation's culture and to explain why, in Japan, both cooperation and freedom are viable and considerateness and vigorous competition are not mutually exclusive.

To make this line of thought feasible, however, two problems must be addressed whose solution will demand some basic revisions in contextual theory. First, the contextual is described entirely in terms that express the individual's attitude toward life: interdependence, mutual trust, the value placed on personal relations in their own right. Cooperation with others or respect for others as actors are frames of mind that an individual is fully capable of possessing as an individual, so with only these prescriptions "contextual" could be merely a different name for a cooperative individual. In fact, both individualism and interdependence rarely appear in pure form; there are obviously many gradations in between. This being the case, the contextual and the individual are neither two different types of social units nor two different modes of human actors; they are simply differences of degree in psychological attitudes.

Qualitative differences distinguishing the contextual from the individual are essential, as is an analysis of the structure that makes the contextual viable qua contextual. In other words, granting that the contextual is one kind of human relationship, it must be explained by delving into the question of what special structure it has that makes it something more than simply relations between individuals on friendly terms. That is, the factors allowing people to be individuals at some times and contextuals at others must be explained not merely in terms of different frames of mind but in terms of inevitable, immovable elements. I tend to lean toward positing a difference in types of human behavior and in structures of behavior, as I will discuss later.

The second problem is that of cultural comparison and the extent to which contextualism is an indigenous Japanese characteristic and the contextual an inevitable unit of Japanese society. Granting a strong tendency toward contextualism in Japanese social history, the question that must be answered is whether this is a basic feature of what the contextualists term this country's "civilization," or only the manifestation in a greater degree of a cultural feature found throughout the world.

Because contextual theory takes a methodological view of the contextual, regarding it as an essential element of society that intervenes between the individual and the whole, I find it inconceivable that its authors intend it to be a narrow theory of Japanese uniqueness. The contextual is a more abstract, universal concept than that of the *ie*, and although it may be largely true that contextualism provided the milieu from which the *ie* emerged, this principle does not pertain only to the *ie*. We must look again at the relationship between the contextual and Japanese culture and the relationship between the Japanese and individualism.

Chapter Five:
Distortions Caused by Modernization

BY now it should be clear
that Japanese society is moved by two coexistent principles
that have supplemented and rivaled each other in the course
of the nation's history. These are the principles of *ie* society and of individualism, of *issho kenmei* and of *ichigo ichie*,
or, to state it more precisely, the organizational principles
of peasants and warriors and the behavioral principles of
merchants. The two have existed side by side without in-
terruption since their inception, the former in the Kamakura
period and the latter in the Muromachi period at the latest,
and each has played an important role not only in the Edo
period but also in the formative decades of the modern age.

Nonetheless, to modern observers the principles of *ie* society undeniably appear predominant, so that they seem to
constitute the pivotal characteristic of Japanese society. As
stated at the outset, the common conception that Japanese culture is basically agrarian is still difficult to shed, and
the idea that it is a warrior's culture was long a widespread
component of the common wisdom, as evidenced by Nitobe
Inazō's *Bushido, the Soul of Japan* (1900). Even worse, as we

have already seen, until a polished theory of *ie* society appeared, Japan tended to be seen simply as a groupist society and at times was even compared to an anthill.

In concluding this study I will briefly outline the reason these stereotypes have held sway, again making a case for individualism and offering some projections of the possible future of Japanese society. Seen in the light of Japan's cultural tradition, the present configuration of society is clearly unnatural. Even viewed from a theoretical standpoint it cannot conceivably be anything more than a very temporary state of affairs. The main factors behind it are two: distortions in the general perception of history and distortions in the nature of industrial society since the Meiji era.

Misapprehension of History

The misperception of history has occurred for some very simple reasons. For one thing, most materials bearing on the history of society and thought have been bequeathed to us by the stable *ie* society. Documents like house rules and organizational charts have been preserved by long-lived *ie*; what is more, the present state of extant *ie* is presumed to testify to their past form. The accomplishments of the people who founded *ie* or the individualists who destroyed them, although they may have been glorious, have generally come down to us only in the form of anecdotes or legends. By contrast, a great many people have participated over extended periods of time in *ie* organizations that have lasted for generations, so naturally many documents and other materials remain. In consequence, organizations

94

have tended to stand out more prominently than individuals in the eyes of modern historians.

Another aspect of the same problem is the approach to history that projects the present onto the past. The problems involved in this way of looking at history have already been mentioned a number of times and need not be repeated here. The reverse process—endeavoring to learn about and interpret the present by seeking its origins in similar phenomena from the past—is, however, a natural attitude that is not entirely off target.

Industrialization and Individualism

We need to address the fundamental question of why the principles of *ie* society have become ascendant and those of individualism declined in modern Japan. Surprisingly, the answer lies in modern industrial society and in the distinctive circumstances of Japan's industrialization. Contrary to common assumption, industrialization is not necessarily fertile ground for individualism; on the contrary, in a way it masks a structure that crushes the individual.

Industrialization centers, of course, on factory production using machines, which by nature divides the production process into planning and execution stages. The artisan creating objects by hand thinks as he works, but the use of machines requires a clear distinction between the stage for thought, when the blueprints are drawn up, and the stage for translating the blueprints into products. The blueprints must be completed before the machines begin operation. Corrections and minute adjustments cannot be made while the machines are running. Machines are a unidirectional means for fulfilling the human will.

In other words, machines separate the hands from the head, giving the head absolute control over the hands. Placed within a factory system, this divides people into two types—those who draft the blueprints and those who turn them into products—who adopt entirely different behavior patterns, at least within the production plant. By and large, the former correspond to managers, product planners, and designers, people who have been granted a far greater opportunity to make full use of their abilities than was possible in premodern times. Using both hands and head, they perform *work* in the planning and design stages that allows them to make use of all their abilities, and the results, produced by machines, are manifested on a grand scale. By contrast, the people who turn the blueprints into products generally correspond to factory laborers, who are reduced to mere hands engaged in monotonous, abstract *labor*. Their labor is subdivided to match the structure of the machines, organized within the framework of a group-based division of labor, as if people were so many machine parts.

Thus, although industrialization enhanced individualism, this merely expanded the potential of one segment of society. The new managers and product designers were more numerous than the nobles and aristocrats of the past and as individuals must have had far greater power to realize their full potential. Thus the quantity of individual ability clearly increased, and it was only natural that individualism took a prominent position in the thinking of the day. At the same time, however, industrialization undeniably deprived many people of the opportunity to make the most of their abilities in their work, submerging their individuality even more than had been the case with the farmers and craftsmen of the past.

This aspect of industrialization has received little attention, probably due mainly to the material abundance that industrialization brought to society and the bigger dreams that it gave laborers of fulfilling their desires, primarily with regard to consumption. Dreams of a better life, however, made laborers more acutely aware of disparities in wealth, causing them to view society from the standpoint of "have nots" versus "haves." This new class consciousness caused people to see only the confrontation between labor and capital and overlook the distinction between labor and work that arose parallel with it. What is more, industrialization destroyed the old peasant and artisan communities, promoting the individuation typical of city life, which may have further expanded the illusion of individualism.

This individualism was but a delusion, however; industrialization eventually produced the human type that has been termed "the masses," which should make it clear that individuation did not create true individuals. Community breakdown produced alienation among laborers, and their dreams of increased consumption only fed their frustration, as Emile Durkheim described in detail long ago in *Suicide*. Both José Ortega y Gasset and David Riesman have pointed out that the more material life improved and superficial freedom expanded, the more people were transformed into "the masses," lacking both pride and the capacity for self-determination.

When this general situation was transplanted to Japan, it involved an even broader spectrum of the population and took on a more intensive form. Japan began industrializing by imitating Western technology and systems and was able to depend on imports for a large portion of the creative work, from management methods to product planning and design. What is more, the West had already created the political systems for operating an industrial society, the social thought to underwrite them, and even educational philosophies to train people for industry, offering models for Japan to imitate. In other words, the plans and goals governing action in early modern Japan were provided almost entirely from the outside; the Japanese needed only to adjust them a bit and accomplish them to the letter. The entire society was transformed into a giant production plant where everyone, including managers and high-level engineers, could be considered essentially a laborer engaged in a group-based division of labor.

The nation was faced with difficult tasks that had to be accomplished without a moment's delay. Not needing to waver over a choice of goals put the so-called modern Japanese in an environment more typical of the peasant or warrior than was any actual peasant or warrior in the past. It was only natural that people placed in such an environment built up their society in *ie* style, intentionally choosing the peasant- and warriorlike aspects of tradition.

Clearly, Japan's industrial society did not adopt *ie* principles and propagate *ie*-like interpersonal relations in the early stages of industrialization. As the authors of *Bunmei to shite no ie shakai* aver, a large proportion of factory laborers in the early Meiji era were hired outside the company structure and had no organizational relationship with management.

Until the beginning of the twentieth century, labor in rapidly expanding companies was provided primarily by unmarried young women from rural communities who were hired for limited periods and by skilled craftsmen under the aegis of a labor contractor (*oyabun*). These people had virtually no feeling of belonging to the company, and the company management had little or no interest in personnel policies affecting them. That is, in early modern industrial companies, laborers were not considered to be members of a quasi-*ie* company organization, and managers were separated from their employees by a gulf not unlike that between the great Tokugawa *ie* and the peasants. The company's relationship with short-term laborers from villages was only temporary, and craftsmen were hired indirectly, through the *oyabun*. This mutual separation and lack of interest resulted in inferior working conditions and high turnover and absentee rates, as well as sporadic escapes and uprisings.

Not until the second decade of the century were laborers finally incorporated into the company, which simultaneously began developing into an *ie*-style organization. Progressive factory mechanization made securing a stable supply of skilled labor essential. At the same time, companies were forced to devise managerial methods to combat the labor-movement ideologies entering from the West. In the 1930s the nation was put on a war footing, which required production increases that made labor morale and loyalty imperative. A sense of unity like that of the *ie* and a philosophy of the "company *ie*" were apt tools for this purpose, and under government guidance business firms enthusiastically pushed measures to make these part of management policy. The foundations of lifetime employment, pay scales based on seniority, corporate welfare plans, enterprise unions, and other features of so-called Japanese management were largely laid during wartime and carried over into the postwar period.

Significantly, the philosophy of socializing and salons was advocated during the transitional decade leading to the advent of the *ie*-style company, but like fireworks, this flared up only to fade away leaving no trace. In 1901 the art critic Iwamura Tōru wrote of his great longing for salons "like the clubs of the West or the cafes of France." In 1909 the novelist Nagai Kafū sharply criticized the atmosphere in industrializing Japan, especially deploring its impoverished social life. A year earlier, the poet Kinoshita Mokutarō and a group of like-minded writers had begun a literary salon, called the Pan Society after the Greek god. This was Japan's first modern cultural salon, but four years later it disbanded and nothing like it ever succeeded again.

Building up the country industrially was the overriding goal of the Japanese government in the early modern period; because industry aimed for an *ie*-type organization, this philosophy naturally enveloped the entire society. Companies gradually grew larger and more numerous, increasing the number of people (including their families) belonging to them. Government agencies and trade unions created organizations resembling those of business firms; and every school in the nation disseminated values that worked to create a social climate that extolled the virtues of living permanently in one place and staying with a single organization and emphasized familistic affinities. This rapidly growing industrial society was a very busy society, one that demanded hard, conscientious, efficient work of people, regardless of what might be going on in their heads. Unlike their Edo-period forebears, the modern Japanese had no time or money to enjoy socializing, and eventually their desire to social-ize waned. Through the prewar and postwar decades this tendency waxed ever stronger, climaxing around the 1970s. To observers at the time, the *ie*-derived values, systems, and customs that then permeated Japanese society appeared to be immutable features of the culture.

The Reawakening of a Dormant Tradition

From this it should be clear that the enormous changes tak-ing place in industrial society today—which some people see as the advent of the postindustrial age, others as sim-ply a more advanced stage of industrialization—will alter Japan's "cultural tradition" tomorrow. Operations in man-ufacturing plants have already changed in ways that are uni-versally apparent, altering human activity accordingly. As machines and plants have been computerized, simple phys-ical labor has been handed over to robots, with more people shifting to jobs related to management, development, and personnel. Diversification of consumer demand is enhancing the importance of invention, planning, design, and services, placing more people in positions involving work as opposed to labor. This trend could heal the split between hands and head that industrialization has caused, also liberating peo-ple from the limitations imposed by the division of labor within organizations and allowing the rebirth of the free, unified being that the individual originally was.

Many other factors in modern society are forcing individuation: The state and social class are losing their ability to control people politically; the centripetal force of the family is weakening for various reasons; tastes and customs have diversified; and longer life spans mean more time spent alone. All these factors diversify and obscure the goals of human behavior, implying situations in every area of life that will obviate the universal utility of an *issho kenmei* approach. People will always have to seek goals for their actions, designing their lives by selecting from among these. This will also mean having to create new interpersonal relationships and maintain them through constant efforts at self-expression. In other words, people will start to live according to the philosophy of *ichigo ichie*, a way of life that I have discussed at length in *Yawarakai kojinshugi no tanjō* (The birth of gentle individualism, 1984).

No matter how much the times change, of course, the past is always with us. Both for the individual and for society as a whole, to live means to master a rhythm; but although a rhythm can contain variations, it cannot withstand a complete break. Thus if the past contains traditions that can be applied to the future, these will enable us to live better. At the same time, as I have said repeatedly, tradition is not something that we are simply given; every age selects its traditions according to its way of life. Selecting a past that has never existed is impossible, of course, but the past is complex and multifaceted and, depending on the way light is shed on it, frequently reveals surprising aspects. This being the case, the past and the present give meaning to and determine each other.

This study has made it clear that Japan is fortunate in having traditions hidden in its past that are suited to helping it ride the changes of the present. Moreover, these are not merely tucked away in historical documents but can, if we change our way of looking at things, be discovered in present-day Japanese life. For example, the method of decision making that is a feature of what is popularly called Japanese-style management can be seen to be a product of the cultural pattern of socializing more than of *ie* mechanisms. Japanese decision making is characterized by careful formation of an agreement that aims for consensus, the importance attached to the formal process toward this end, and the nurturing of empathy that transcends logical persuasion—the methods of social salons the world over. It is common knowledge that Japanese business life always involves a prodigious number of occasions for eating, drinking, and other forms of conviviality within the organization and that the *nemawashi* for important decisions frequently takes place over drinks in the evening.

In view of the true nature of socializing, the problem here obviously lies in these activities being limited to the company organization, closing it to the outside. The original, premodern *ie*, too, involved a wide variety of self-contained, private socializing activities that in fact underwrote its characteristics as an *ie*. The fundamental difference from the modern pattern is simply that in premodern times a great variety of salons existed outside the *ie*, and by belonging to a number of these, people could escape the confinement of the *ie* organization.

This being the case, the cultural patterns of Japanese socializing may merely have been distorted by modernization and may be quietly living on even now in the Japanese psyche. If the sensibilities of Japanese decision making could be liberated from the confinement of *ie*-type organizations, they could well turn into an effective principle for forming the order of the future, not only in Japan but throughout the world. For example, the so-called networking principle as explained by the American writers Jessica Lipnack and Jeffrey Stamps is clearly underwritten by a Japanese-style sense of consensus formation. At long last, at the end of the twentieth century, with talk of the postmodern period in the air, the cosmopolitan nature of Japanese culture could be demonstrated once again. Whether this happens will, of course, depend on how the Japanese live in the future.

PART II

THE UNIVERSALITY OF GENTLE INDIVIDUALISM

Chapter Six:
Culture and Individuation

Any attempt to define the unique characteristics of a given culture contains an inherent dilemma, the perilous logical pitfall of trying to assign unique features to each of the world's many different cultures.

Because a unique characteristic is, obviously, a quality without parallel that serves to distinguish one entity from all others, people who talk about unique cultural features try to ascribe the deepest possible significance to the absence of comparable features in other cultures. They stress that a small discrepancy in outward appearance is actually the manifestation of some essential difference, a matter of qualitative disparity rather than of quantitative variation. In those who concern themselves with cultural uniqueness, this point of view is understandable. At the same time, however, a culture is an assertion of values, the comprehensive picture of what, for the people living in that culture, are universal standards that should receive widespread affirmation. The habits and customs of the individual do not become culture, even for that person, until they are accepted widely enough that they can be imposed upon others through coercion or persuasion.

This being the case, stressing the unique characteristics of a culture means asserting the universality of features that have no parallel. Taken to its logical conclusion, this leads to problems because it requires assuming either that only one entity in the world has unique features or that there are many universal value standards—a difficult proposition in either case. Both traditional cultural imperialism and the cultural relativism advocated by the new wave of anthropologists are approaches that reflect this dilemma.

Imperialist and Relativist Views of Culture

Whether consciously or unconsciously, premodern views of culture tended to be imperialistic. Both Western cultures, beginning with ancient Greece, and Eastern cultures, most notably imperial China, believed that their own way of life had an intrinsic worth found nowhere else in the world and that imposing it on others was perfectly acceptable. They saw themselves as the sole repository of culture, regarding everything beyond their borders as a cultural void, a barbaric expanse to be contemptuously ignored or forcibly "enlightened." Even in modern times this classical view of culture lived on in the West, serving to justify missionary work among colonized peoples and armed conflict between ethnic groups.

In many cases this attitude still lurks in the background of oft-repeated assumptions about Japanese culture. People who consider Japanese culture to be group oriented, as op-

posed to Western culture, which they see as being individualistic, are frequently guilty of tacitly assuming that
individualism is a feature unique to Western culture and, at
the same time, that the individual is generally closer to the
essential nature of humanity than is the group. It stands
to reason, then, that because the essential nature of humanity is universal, and universality is vital to culture, Western
individualism is culturally superior to Japan's groupism.

This self-righteous assumption of Western cultural superiority must have lain hidden in the depths of Ruth
Benedict's mind when, during World War II, she wrote *The
Chrysanthemum and the Sword*, positing Japanese culture
as being based on a sense of shame developing out of a group
orientation in contrast to Western culture, which she
described as being characterized by feelings of guilt deriving from the individual's awareness of self. The simple and
obvious logical fallacy in this view of culture is that if a
given cultural feature is a manifestation of the universal
essence of human nature, its presence will not be limited
to a single culture.

Concepts of whole numbers, of direction, and of size have
broad enough applicability to be considered universal, and
all cultures have in fact shared them from the outset. If a
given cultural feature is indeed rooted in the essence of human nature, the potential for it to exist must be intrinsic
to all cultures, even though it may be in evidence in one
culture but not in another. The apparent disparity between
the two cultures is then merely a difference in the degree
to which some element manifests itself, a variation in the
overall balance between this and other features of the
cultures.

This brings to mind a delightful exchange between some zealous Western missionaries who came to Japan in the mid-sixteenth century and the Japanese they sought to convert. The missionaries preached that the Christian God was the eternal and universal truth, as if this should be obvious to anyone, and strove to enlighten the people to his teachings. The Japanese responded by questioning why, if this were an eternal truth, they had not known it from the start but had to be taught about it for the first time at this stage of their history.

Diametrically opposed to this imperialistic view of culture stands the bulk of modern cultural anthropology, which strives to resolve the same dilemma by taking the reverse approach. Whereas cultural imperialism places extreme emphasis on the universality of one culture's characteristics, consequently repudiating different features found in other cultures, modern anthropology attempts to acknowledge the special attributes of all cultures as equally valid.

Seen from this viewpoint, the culture of a single African tribe is equal in value and potential universality to European culture as a whole. Apart from physical measures, such as economic wealth or military power, the yardstick of value lies within a given culture, and cross-cultural gauges of relative superiority do not and cannot exist.

This means that the universality of values is limited to the confines of a given culture; across cultural bounds all values become relative. Not only have modern anthropologists adopted this stance in opposition to imperialistic cultural invasion, they have also frequently used it as a basis for casting doubt on excessive modernization of indigenous ways of life.

The logical simplicity of this viewpoint and the way it harmonizes with modern ethnic sentiment have won it acceptance as an ideal perspective to bring to official international negotiating tables. Regarded in purely theoretical terms, however, this view of culture is predicated on a definitive internal contradiction that obviously makes it unsatisfactory as a philosophy of culture. That is, it fails to provide guidelines for stipulating the size of the unit referred to as "a culture" or for establishing grounds on which to determine the degree to which such a unit is independent of other cultures.

A nation or an ethnic group is commonly considered a single cultural unit. In fact, however, the collectivity referred to as "nation" is artificial and arbitrary, while by scientific standards "ethnic group" is nothing more than a vague notion. The regional cultures within nations, the tribal cultures within ethnic groups, and the cultures of towns, villages, and even smaller community groupings, down to individual families, are all legitimately qualified to be counted as cultural units.

By the same token, if an issue is to be made of cultural invasion between nations, nations must be taken to task for intruding upon the local cultures within their borders, and local communities must be held responsible for absorbing family culture. Exhaustive refinement of the conditions defining cultural independence leads ultimately to the habits and customs of the individual, at which point the concept of culture breaks down. In the final analysis, cultural relativism relativizes culture itself, thereby negating the concept of culture.

Recognizing the validity of the concept of culture means

accepting that a culture is an entity that strives for a certain degree of universality and extends itself by influencing other cultures, even fusing with them at times. At the same time, however, cultures are entitled to have divergent distinguishing characteristics, and when our own culture is subjected to outside interference, we are displeased, at the very least. Another aspect of this straightforward emotion, however, is that it relates directly to pride in the universality of our own culture, leading to unconscious expansionism; this renders the dilemma faced by culture theory serious indeed.

Individuation as a Precultural Principle

To resolve this dilemma, it is necessary to direct attention away from narrowly defined culture theory and seek not for the attributes and universalities present in specific cultures but for the fundamental principles that precede and give rise to all cultures.

If such principles exist, their very existence functions as the principle by which values are universalized, mediating the universalization process between individual cultures without impairing these cultures' integrity. The problem is more amenable to solution if one culture's expansion and fusion with another is not regarded as a matter of the characteristics of the former being more universal than those of the latter; instead, this process should be considered the result of the expanded culture's having adhered more closely to universal principles antecedent to both cultures. These "precultural" principles are, obviously, subliminally present in every culture. Cultural fusion, therefore, is not a matter of one culture's assimilating features of another but of something in the other culture stimulating the full flowering of aspects already present in the first. Although one culture may act as a stimulus or catalyst for changes in another, in terms of basic principle no culture can invade or subjugate another.

Naturally, it is difficult to isolate concrete examples of those aspects of human works and ways that precede culture. By the time they are manifested in human living, even phenomena that are considered to be instinctive or biological include such deep-seated cultural influences that they are no longer simply natural phenomena. If, however, humans have created culture from elements found in nature, in doing so they must have followed a number of basic principles—principles that logically precede culture.

Humans are believed to possess such concepts as whole numbers and basic modes of perception before they experience anything at all. Needless to say, such concepts existed before culture came into being. Without the concepts of up and down or left and right humans would not arrange things spatially; likewise, basic numerical concepts must exist before people can measure quantities in terms of numbers. Suppose a culture existed that lacked any developed concept of number and people referred to all numbers over two as simply "a lot." If these people knew that "a lot" means anything from three upward, their culture would possess latent numerical concepts. Similar precultural principles that immediately spring to mind include rules of formal logic and Noam Chomsky's innate-language theory, but further consideration should reveal, even among more empirical principles, some unexpected examples of principles that precede culture.

The suggestion that individuation is one of these principles may arouse strong misgivings in many people. Needless to say, the concept of individuation relates to modern-day individualism and tends to be regarded as the product of historical processes within a specific culture, namely, modern Western culture. Positing the principle of individuation as a force creating culture as such may engender suspicions that this argument leads ultimately to acceptance of the superiority of Western culture, thus serving as an apology for antiquated imperialism.

Although modern Western individualism may well have arisen from the principle of individuation, the reverse is obviously not true: The principle of individuation cannot have emerged from individualism. The tendency toward individuation is rooted deep in history, in the drive to preserve individual units of life, which conceivably antedates not only culture but even the biological origins of humankind.

In the precultural state this drive was exercised in perfect balance with the drive to preserve the species. The preservation of the individual could not have been an end in itself or have taken precedence over the need to maintain the species. The life and death of the individual were built into the dialectical process through which the life of the species developed, and the attendant joys and sorrows must have been inextricably intertwined with the species' prosperity.

Eventually the moment came when the individual took a step toward making itself an end and began living for the sake of its own joy in life. This can be seen as the instant when culture first departed from nature. In the course of using fire to process food, for example, if at some point humans began to cook food to improve its taste rather than simply to make it hygienic or preserve it, this must have been the origin of cooking as a cultural phenomenon. If at some point the formation of a family ceased to mean merely that parents nurtured their young in the same way as animals but also meant that children took care of their aged parents, this must have been the birth of cultural sentiments. Both the quest for tasty food and the protection of the elderly infirm can at times be detrimental from the standpoint of preserving the species, but they are indispensable to the happiness of the individual. Along with these undertakings for the well-being of the individual, humans began to create a world of their own—culture—that conflicted with nature.

Sacrificial offerings were among the earliest practices instituted when magical religion was taking shape as a cultural form. This can be viewed as humanity's first awakening to the significance of individual life. Human sacrifice was a manifestation not of disregard for individual life but, in fact, of its direct opposite: Such ceremonies pray for the resurrection of a larger body of life in exchange for the sacrifice of an individual unit of life, a negotiation that is possible only if the life of the individual takes on importance equal to that of the species.

The classicist Gilbert Murray and some anthropologists hold that these sacrificial offerings subsequently produced the archetype of dramatic tragedy, that the sacred beast on the altar developed into the tragic hero who dies on the stage. If their thesis is accepted, this can be seen as the point at which the principle of biological individuation produced the first "individual."

The tragic hero of ancient Greece was still destined to die for the life of his species. As an individual he was simultaneously both mighty and powerless, the paragon of intelligence and wisdom but utterly benighted in the face of fate. Gradually, however, the individuating aspect of this double-faceted being intensified until, more than two millenniums later, it has been transformed into the almighty modern individual.

With the birth of culture, humankind began believing in a soul and devising various ceremonies to pray for its eternal life. This is also evidence that the individual had begun to dissociate itself from the life of the species. For humankind at this juncture, the life of the species was eternal, so there should have been no need to pray for its immortality, and individual beings who were completely immersed in it would have had no particular reason to seek eternity for the soul. The fear of death was unquestionably the first emotion that human beings recognized when they became aware of themselves as individuals, creating the need to allay this fear by praying for repose in the afterworld. A desire for eternal youth also emerged parallel with this, and there should be no need to elaborate on its tremendous contribution to the formation of culture.

Education is another of the earliest undertakings associated with culture and the most salient evidence that life gave rise to independent beings. Education began when offspring, separated from the parents physiologically, were no longer able to survive with only the genetic information and instincts they had been born with—that is, when the information received directly from the life of the species became inadequate for the individual's survival and the individual felt the need for acquired information. The advent of education commemorated the individual's perceived need for active self-development in order to survive and the beginning of demand for independent endeavor to that end. This meant, however, that maintaining the life of the species came to depend on the effort of the individual, putting the key to the species' existence into the individual's hands and bringing the power of the individual and of the species much closer to parity.

The dawn of education gave the individual a second maturation process, one based on acquired knowledge. In addition to its original physiological maturation, leading to the birth of the next generation, the individual advanced through stages of accomplishment in which it acquired various skills and symbols. These new stages were established independently, outside the life of the individual, eventually becoming an ordered system with a structure of its own that outlived the individual. From the perspective of the life of the species, the quantity of information needed for living expanded, spilling over into the realm outside life, where it came to form a whole in its own right, creating a second life of the species. For the individual this meant envelopment in two wholes that it both contributed to and depended on: this second structure—which, in its totality, is what we call culture—in addition to the life of the species.

Education, the offering of sacrifices, belief in the spirit, the quest for tasty food, and the custom of caring for parents have characterized every ethnic group since the earliest stages of human culture. Given that all of these began with the individual's independence—and awareness of its independence—from the life of the species, the hypothesis that the individuation of life is a universal principle in the establishment of culture is fairly well verified. Moreover, because the principle of individuation is the force that once separated humans from the natural world and created culture, humans cannot evade it. If this principle is to be called individualism in the broadest sense, humans have been unable to escape the desire to be individualistic since the formative stage of culture. Oedipus, who schemed to thwart fate; the ancient Chinese emperors, who sought eternal youth; the Buddha, who wished to break out of the cycle of transmigration—all were individualists in the broad sense. This line of thought makes it necessary to revise radically our suppositions about the significance both of the various changes that have taken place in modern culture and of reciprocal influences between cultures.

For example, the securing of political freedom and economic equality, the implementation of social welfare measures pertaining to medical treatment and care for the weak and infirm, the development of the nuclear family and widespread family planning, the guarantee of human rights bearing on religious freedom and occupational choice, and the fostering of the kind of industrial production base that underwrites these have, until now, been considered to be among the cultural features distinguishing a modern society. These have been thought of as the products of the individualistic philosophies that have emerged in Western society since the eighteenth century in the context of the distinctive features of Judaic and Hellenic culture, including monotheism and idealistic philosophy. It has been assumed that modernization was a phenomenon that began within Western culture and that its global spread resulted from the power of Western nations.

In the light of the new perspective outlined above, however, the various tendencies of modern society can be viewed as products of the precultural principle of biological individuation, the direct outgrowth of the fundamental principles that produce culture and make it what it is. In other words, the core of modernization is a stage that all cultures are destined to reach.

From the standpoint of these fundamental principles, no ethnic nationalistic movement can resist modernization in this sense. Ethnicism is in fact an individuation movement, based on the same principle as modernization, that protects the ethnic group in question by excluding other groups. Paradoxically, however, when carried through, this inevitably gives rise to countless movements on the part of individuals that splinter the group's own ranks. We have witnessed such a case in China's ethnocentric Cultural Revolution and the backlash of the ensuing modernization movement.

Culture and Society as Dynamic Processes

This rather abstract discussion has provided two fundamental perspectives to bring to bear on the examination of culture theory. The first is that culture is by no means a fixed entity, but a set of dynamic processes of generation and transformation. The other is that individualism in its narrow, historical sense should be distinguished from the universal principle of individuation, which transcends culture.

Because the primary meaning of culture is the cultivation of nature—activity creating a world dissociated from the wild—the essence of culture is obviously an endless series of dynamic processes, and culture remains culture only while these processes are in motion, so that it is essentially progressive. As I see it, individuation is one of the pivots of this progress, and a fair portion of the differences that have historically marked individual cultures can be viewed as variations in the degree and modality of individuation.

At the same time, culture cannot be progressive in the simplest sense of the term. Nature must exist if it is to be cultivated; unilateral overcultivation that destroys nature ultimately spells death for culture itself. In the context of the present discussion, the life of the individual is ultimately part of the life of the species, so that even if the individual asserts itself, it cannot do so to the extent of negating the continued existence of the species. If, for example, everyone exercised the individual's freedom not to have children, humankind would disappear within a few decades, leaving nobody to assert this kind of freedom. The deep paradox of culture is that even as it works ceaselessly for self-realization, it is destined to collapse if it fails to maintain regard for the natural world from which it is created.

This dialectic lends even greater dynamism to the motion of culture, generating a kind of paradox at every evolutionary stage. Throughout history, the advance of individuation has frequently produced side effects that have eventually reinforced the life of the species in surprising ways. Although the quest for eternal youth has never attained its goal, it has spurred advances in medicine that have contributed to increasing the human population. Protection of the weak and respect for the souls of the dead have ameliorated the animallike competition for survival of the fittest, aiding the formation of the peace and order necessary to the continued existence of groups. Meanwhile, the spread of the modern nuclear family and family planning, while directly responsible for population decline, have facilitated more thorough education of individuals, thereby raising society's productive capacity.

In modern times the individual's activity has been diversifying and group membership become more pluralistic, thereby diminishing occupational and interest groups' control over their members. But depending on how it is viewed, even this extreme individuation can be considered to produce a paradoxical effect. As the individual undertakes activity in a number of arenas, the benefits the individual seeks also multiply. In other words, desires and intentions proliferate and diversify. Belonging to a number of groups means that the individual takes on multiple identities; weakening the group's capacity for control and the individual's sense of loyalty to the group mean less persistence in individual ideology. This leads to the conjecture that by thus creating plural identities, that is, by destroying the unity of the individual as an individual and creating invisible others within the self, individuation opens up new possibilities for cooperation with others.

Viewing culture as a dynamic process means attributing greater dynamism than has previously been assumed both to a single culture and society and to the principles underlying their structure. In short, it is necessary to stop viewing society as a collection of specific structural elements and to perceive it instead as the state of balance between two types of motion—individuation and unification—like the balance between wave and particle motion in light theory.

Although difficult to visualize from a common-sense perspective, individuals and organizations do not exist first as firm units whose movement creates society; the dynamics of society exist first, creating individuals and groups that take on the role of actor depending on the occasion. To say that the dynamics of society exist first is, of course, merely a convenient expression. Strictly speaking, initially there is only the discord between the principles of individuation and preservation of the species, and society is created as the tentative actor carrying out the motion deriving from this tension. Provided that it is only for the sake of convenience, speaking of the individual as the subject of action is, of course, also acceptable. In this case too, however, a preexisting individual does not initiate social action; a specific type of action and the appropriate attitude for it exist first and create the actor in the form of the individual.

Sociology has long struggled with the question of whether the individual exists prior to society, which is formed only when individuals come together, or, conversely, society is the preexisting entity of which the individual merely perceives itself to be a constituent element. This controversy has now been superseded, however, by the view that invisible principles and dynamics precede and create both society and the individual. Strange as this idea may seem, the ambiguity of the concepts of society and individual should make it clear that it conforms to reality.

The Meaning of "Individual"

Society is commonly considered to be a collection of independent individual beings; an undifferentiated amoeba-like aggregation does not constitute a society. Although animal and plant cells are certainly alive individually they congregate to form not a society of cells but a separate animal or plant.

The term "society" is applied figuratively to animals, such as ants or monkeys, and there is even a discipline called animal sociology, but for some reason "society" is not used to describe a cluster of plants. In everything from a clump of cells through an amoebic aggregation to a cluster of plants or a group of animals, although the difference is merely one of the degree of individuation, the unit of reference has sometimes been an individual body and sometimes a society.

That the distinction between the two is so vague indicates that society and the individual are not entities but names given to different aspects of a state of flux. The discord between the life of the species and its individuation exists prior to all else, and both society and the individual can be viewed as no more than byproducts of the process that creates a state of balance between them in a number of stages.

The attempt to distinguish the individual as a unit of humanity from an individual biological being or a single physical item immediately renders the independence of that unit unclear. Ordinarily an individual is thought of as an entity that acts spontaneously in accordance with specific desires, intentions, and tastes and maintains its identity through memory and introspection. In reality, however, no such human being exists. Desires and tastes are easily influenced by the group, making it impossible for a person to act purely spontaneously, and no person preserves a complete inner identity in the psychological dimension. No matter how passionately a person may hope for world peace, in the psychological dimension that wish may be momentarily forgotten, and other problems will frequently set the person's heart burning with different desires. The person is a pacifist as an individual not because of incessant praying for peace but by virtue of holding a particular worldview that provides a point of reference to return to when necessary, regardless of the person's psychological state. A viewpoint must be a position that theoretically can be taken by anyone. In fact, a particular position becomes strong when it is broadly enough defined for anyone to hold and when it is shared by groups that may or may not have clear parameters.

Paradoxically, the individual maintains its self-identity most strongly when it belongs to a powerful group of like-minded people and devotes itself most faithfully to the solidarity of that group. The same applies in a slightly different form to desires, intentions, and tastes, establishing the paradox that the person's individuality is generally identical with that person's sharing in the life of the group.

The individual does not exist intrinsically but comes into being through the assertion and the expression of the self. The formless energy that touches off and sustains such assertion and expression exists prior to the individual. In its visible forms, this energy appears as various ready-made assertions or expressions that invite people to join in the viewpoints being represented, which may include traditional values, the spirit of the times, political ideology, various norms of religion and folk belief, or popular morals and tastes. These precede the birth of the individual and function as the principles by which a society unifies itself, that is, the social principles of preservation of the species.

People may readily choose, from among the manifestations of invisible energy confronting them, those viewpoints that they will adopt as their own, or they may feel the urge to reject what is presented and create different viewpoints of their own. In either case, making a choice is what first brings the individual into being.

In the former case, the individual obviously comes into being through belonging to the group, but in the latter case, provided that the new viewpoint is also universally valid, the individual now belongs to a new group that as yet lacks a definite form. Something has certainly been created, but not out of nothing as if by magic. Some visible, established worldview or set of values has inspired the individual to rebel and create a new viewpoint, in that moment articulating the mood of an era that cannot yet be seen but is larger than the old, established perspective, which it also includes.

Before actively choosing a position, the human is still a semiconscious biological being, dimly aware of belonging to and drifting with the mood of the times. At this stage the principles of individuation and preservation of the species are in balance at a low level; the individuality of the human being is vague, but at the same time, the energy that gives rise to grouping is not yet strong or directed. Eventually, however, the needs inherent in the principle of preservation of the species cause the force that propels grouping to intensify and to endeavor to mobilize all segments of the group in a common direction. If grouping is to be enhanced, the group must be given a clear outline and be drawn toward a gravitational center. This, however, brings about paradoxical results from the standpoint of the life of the species: Restricting the size of the group will, obviously, strengthen its centripetal force, but it also immediately implies the division and pluralization of the species.

Furthermore, although this centripetal force should become even stronger when each segment of the group is imbued with energy that actively draws it toward the center, each part's having energy of its own sets the individuation process in motion within the group. To put it more concretely, human society has stronger unity when it is created through the convergence of autonomous wills than when it is a congeries of slaves, but at the same time, exercising the will leads to the free individual's independence from the group.

In this way the principle of preservation of the species negates itself in order to strengthen itself, paradoxically turning to the principle of individuation. The individual, unique to humankind, came into being when these two principles attained a certain stage of balance.

This was, simultaneously, the awakening of human consciousness. The conscious has no substance, of course, and it is not the entirety of the individual. Consciousness is a function, a process of unending motion that, while constantly shutting the individual's inner self off from the external world, also opens it up to the external world at every point where it is closed off.

For example, the vague mood of an era that exists in the external world may at some point be clearly demarcated and incorporated by the conscious; when this becomes a lucid image, it molds the individual's inner self. At this moment the conscious certainly appears to be synonymous with the individual, and the clearly demarcated internal self seems to be closed to the nebulous outside world. In the next instant, however, the conscious further crystallizes this image into a concept that it then articulates as a worldview, a position, which at that point becomes a part of the world that is external to the conscious. This worldview continues to exist when the conscious is dormant and is also public property that many consciousnesses can share. This brings us back to what was said earlier: The individual becomes an individual by virtue of incorporating participation in the public realm.

Just as the principle of preservation of the species negates itself in order to manifest itself, so too does the principle of individuation. The individual comes into being only in the context of a state of balance between these opposing principles.

The Inevitability and Limitations of the Modern Individual

This approach permits a fresh understanding of so-called rugged, modern individualism and its historical limitations. Modern individualism is a view of humanity that justifies inner beliefs and unilateral self-assertion, as well as competition based on these. This philosophy underwrites everything in the West in modern times, from politics to art, and has spread throughout the world along with industrialization. In principle it must be acknowledged that the global spread of this view of humanity was only natural and at one time was prevalent over other perspectives. At the same time, however, we need to realize that this type of individualism is not a characteristic specific to Western culture, that it does not embody eternal truth and justice, and that this version is not the only form that individualism can take.

To think otherwise means accepting the inevitability of modernization and recognizing cultural progress only within a limited scope. Because the principle of individuation precedes culture and is the main driving force in its formation, every culture in the world is destined to pass through a stage of simple individualism.

Modern individualism is based on a naive naturalism and springs from a common-sense view of the individual as being identical to the physical individual being. This view of humankind extends from the impulse to protect only one's own physical self that arises almost reflexively when the physiological human being senses that pain and pleasure are felt by the self alone and cannot be shared with others. This is a simplistic line of thought, but as long as modern humankind, as a biological organism, lives and strikes a balance between maintenance of the individual and of the species at this level, fundamental refutation of modern individualism remains difficult. This situation may change, of course, if, at some future time, the duration of childhood were drastically lengthened and education gained greater importance than instinct in preserving the species, causing a revolutionary increase in the individual's dependence on others. In the meantime, however, a view of humanity that places priority on the welfare of the corporeally individualized individual and desires its safety and happiness will continue spreading throughout the world as a spirit of the times that every culture experiences at least once.

It should be unnecessary to elaborate further on the impossibility of claiming that individualism is unique to Western culture. The principle of individuation has manifested itself with varying speeds and in different forms in different geographical locations and social groups.

The cultural stress on guilt described by Ruth Benedict—in which the individual explains the self in terms of awareness of guilt and feels that passing judgment on the self preserves the individual's independence—is most probably a characteristic peculiar to the West. By contrast, as discussed in Chapters Two and Three, Japanese people perceive the self as having *shin*, sincerity or good faith, and endeavor to preserve the dignity of the self by conducting their lives in keeping with *shin*. Similarly, this is a characteristic specific to Japanese culture.

The most we can say about these features as the distinguishing characteristics of cultures, however, is that whereas Western culture embraces the pessimistic concept of guilt, Japanese culture embraces the optimistic concept of sincerity. Underlying both is the individual's awakening to the dignity of the self, which is rooted in universal principles that precede culture.

Part I examined Japanese culture's tradition of individualism in the broad sense. This has presented some types of individuals who come close to the modern image and others who transcend it. The resemblance to one aspect of Western culture is no mere coincidence; it is not unique to Japanese culture but is merely evidence that Japanese culture is one culture among many and has a history worthy of a culture.

No two ideas could be further apart than the concept that modern individualism will inevitably be experienced at some time in a culture's history and the notion that modern individualism is an eternal truth and ethically correct. The latter view is supported both by conventional sociological theory and by the preconception that society is established on the basis of the congregation of substantive entities called individuals: If the individual exists prior to society and is considered the essence of society, then it stands to reason that society should ideally be in a state in which this essence has fully materialized. This leads to the conclusions that the total immersion of the individual in the group, as seen in the past, was a distorted form of society and that history progressed in a straight line until the birth of the modern individual brought it to its culmination.

This view of society is, however, basically flawed. As has already been clarified, society is not a congregation of substantive individuals and history cannot progress in a straight line. The modern individual gives the appearance of being a substantive entity, but in fact it is merely a phenomenon appearing in the West from the seventeenth to the mid-twentieth century and has generally been nothing more than the modality of an era brought on by industrialization. In fact, in the latter half of the twentieth century the individual has been showing signs of fissioning as a consequence of the individuation process, revealing itself to be little more than a conglomeration of relationships to which it belongs on the basis of a variety of viewpoints and interests—in other words, a composite of a number of identities.

Another context within which the individual is manifested is what the German sociologist Georg Simmel has termed *Geselligkeit*, probably best rendered in English as "socializing" or "fraternizing," a form of activity unique to humankind. In this context the individual, while remaining an individual, manifests itself in a totally different state. Regarded even from a superficial perspective, socializing is a form of pleasurable entertainment in which firmly held convictions and passionate desires have little place. Since relations with other people constitute the essence of socializing, it is not conducive to unilateral self-assertion and competition with others. Nonetheless, even after the emergence of the modern individual, people have enthusiastically taken part in socializing, suppressing their everyday selves and setting aside their viewpoints and assertions to enjoy conversation. People know that this does not mean completely suppressing the individual, and they tacitly recognize socializing as another manifestation of individualism.

Chapter Seven:
Socializing and Socialization

CONTEXTUALISM, a theory formulated by Hamaguchi Eshun and Kumon Shumpei, incisively pinpoints the shortcomings of modern individualism and offers an alternative model of human existence.

This theory has already been discussed in detail in Chapter Four. To recapitulate briefly, first of all, a small group is placed between society as a whole and the individual, serving to mediate between the two. This group has attributes of its own, just as if it were an individual, and behaves as a unified actor in the same way that the individual does. The term "contextual" is used to express this concept. To borrow an image from physics, the individual is to the contextual as the atom is to the molecule. Like the molecule in the physical world, the contextual is the main actor in various social phenomena. A society's distinctive behavioral patterns and customs initially appear in the contextual. These are considered to eventually prescribe the distinguishing features of the society as a whole and the specific cultural characteristics of the individual, as well. Contextualism, thus, aims for a hypostatic solution to the classic sociological debate over whether the individual or society is the true state of human existence. It attempts to explain the essential nature of society by proposing that what really exists is an intermediate category—a very clear and simple compromise.

Secondly, contextualism focuses on Japanese culture in particular, emphasizing that the contextual way of life is a prominent characteristic of Japanese society. Contextual theory holds that individualists are egocentric, relying on themselves and seeing relations with others as a means, whereas contextualists, valuing interdependence and mutual trust, consider relationships between the self and others to be the essence of human existence. The latter view of life is said to be distinctively Japanese.

The Contextual and the Individual

Contextual theory is based on verifiable observation of society and looks at the behavioral modes of the small group as actor in a wide range of interpersonal relations, from the modern Japanese workplace to traditional patterns of behavior in so-called *ie* society. The Japanese word for "human being," *ningen* (人 間), is written with ideograms meaning "between people," and according to Hamaguchi, even in the most ordinary usage it implies, to the Japanese, a relationship (*aidagara*) between people. Hamaguchi coined the word *kanjin* (間 人), or "contextual," by simply reversing the two ideograms of *ningen*.

As has already been said, the main motivation for creating the contextual theory was to defend Japanese culture and, to this end, criticize modern individualistic thought—in which it has achieved considerable success. Interestingly enough, in placing the small group midway between the individual and society as a whole, this theory resembles the criticism that early modern Western philosophers leveled against the individualism of their own day. In *L'Ancien régime*, the nineteenth-century French historian Alexis de Tocqueville pointed to the misfortune brought about when the French Revolution destroyed the traditional small community, setting the nation and the individual in direct conflict. Another Frenchman, the sociologist Émile Durkheim, contended in *Suicide* that modernization ruined the craft guilds and other close-knit groups, robbing the individual of a stable situation in which it knew its proper place, thereby causing the insecurity found among people in the modern era.

A person's position within a group definitely grows more conceptual and abstract the larger the group becomes. In too large a group the faces of the other members become indistinct and behavior can be directed only toward the abstract world at large. When behavior is oriented toward this sort of abstract object over too great a distance, it is probably only natural that self-assertion becomes exaggerated and rigid. There is uncertainty over whether the message will be received, and the absence of any visible response makes it difficult to fine-tune the assertion.

History demonstrates all too clearly how easily modern individuals have obfuscated their position and declaimed banal philosophies when they have belonged to a large group, such as nation, race, or class. Paradoxically, the totalitarian movements fascism, Nazism, and communism all arose in the West in modern times, crushing the individual more than did any medieval power holder—a highly suggestive historical lesson. As a criticism of civilization, contextual theory hits the mark when it censures modern Western culture by taking the presence of the small group in society as the theory's pivotal premise and admonishing individualism for lacking this group.

Nonetheless, as an enterprising social theory contextualism, like all theories, undeniably contains a number of flaws that cannot be ignored. A couple of these have already been mentioned. Of particular concern here is the attempt to defend Japanese culture on the basis of the contextualist argument regarding the essential structure of society.

Contextualism likens the contextual to the individual as a component element of society, asserting that the contextual is a truer form of existence than the individual and that theoretically, as well, it better explains the relationship between society and its parts. This line of thought, however, brings contextual theory close to the very reductionism it criticizes, putting it in danger of making the same mistake committed by modern individualism in the past. What is more, having made these assertions, the contextualists claim that the contextual has developed to perfection in Japanese society, shaping the characteristics of Japanese culture, a line of thought that seems likely to lead to a chauvinistic self-adulation reminiscent of past ideas of Western cultural superiority. It raises concern over resurgence of the argument that since Japanese society is a contextual society and contextual society is the essential form of human society, all other societies are deficient and backward.

Naturally, contextual theory is not reductionist in the

simplest sense. Its authors explain that the contextual has a unique, flexible structure; that, unlike the individual, it is divisible; and that it is a distinctive element incorporating the character of society as a whole. According to Hamaguchi, the contextual is a variant of the holon as described by Arthur Koestler: If you look inward it is a self-contained independent whole, while if you look outward, it is just a subordinate part of society as a whole. In other words, it is a unit best described as a "sub-whole, sub-individual." This is a carefully thought out explanation, and if such an element or unit exists, the relationship between the whole and its parts can be neatly explained without contradiction.

When this theory is examined in the light of actual social structure, however, two major problems become apparent. The first is the question of why the qualification to become a "sub-whole" or "sub-individual" is limited to the small group called the contextual and does not exist in the individual. The second is that of what kind of energy produces this special unit, whether a contextual or an individual. To be specific, what way of life and behavior qualifies a unit as a holon of society?

The first problem seems to derive from contextual theory's overemphasis on the significance of the small group, which gives the theory some rather narrow biases regarding the individual that have caused it from the outset to see the individual as overly closed and isolated. If this qualification is only a matter of the part containing the character of the whole, that part need not necessarily be the small group. This capacity was attributed even to the "monad," the indivisible smallest particle, formulated by the seventeenth-century metaphysicist Gottfried Leibniz. The individual, with its great capacity for sympathy and empathy, is far better equipped to become a part of the whole at any time. I have already expressed my suspicion that the characteristics attributed to the contextual—mutual reliance, interdependence, and seeing interpersonal relationships as having intrinsic value—are nothing more than attitudes that the individual can also adopt.

More importantly, as discussed earlier, the individual is definitely not an indivisible entity; it is merely an aggregate of diverse viewpoints, the conjunction of the numerous relationships to which it belongs. The individual is indivisible in the biological sense, but this is certainly not the issue when it is considered as a basic element of society. To postulate that the contextual is open vis-à-vis society while the individual is a closed and complete entity results from unconscious identification of the individual with the physical being, which could invite the charge that contextualism is just another version of the reductionism of modern individualism.

The second issue—that of the kind of energy that produces a holonistic unit—is in some ways the more essential one. It also involves the question of whether divisibility and internal aggregation are sufficient for a part to be harmonious with the whole. To put it another way, this is the question of whether any group is capable of becoming a holonistic constituent of society if only it is a specific group in which mutual dependence and reliance are established.

This problem actually contains some very realistic implications and relates to the basic doubts that have been raised about the egotism of modern business, the family, and various interest groups. In the case of a fighting group that works efficiently in pursuit of a goal, the more loyal the constituent members are to their fellows, the more exclusive the behavior of the group frequently becomes with respect to those outside it. In other words, the more that people within a group adopt a contextual attitude, the more closed the group becomes toward society as a whole—frequently even more so than the individualistic individual. This, paradoxically, is the situation with Japanese groupism, the trait of Japanese society that Western individualists criticize and that contextual theory is trying to defend.

In theoretical terms, this indicates that what makes the contextual really a contextual is neither just its tendency to congregate nor the importance it places on interdependence, mutual reliance, and relationships with others, which are simply frames of mind. It also shows that although the Japanese may be innately gentle and tolerant, this psychological character does not make Japanese society a holonistic whole. Of course attitudes make a contextual what it is, but these must be more than simply subjective frames of mind—they must be backed up by an objective behavioral structure. If the contextual is the creation of a particular behavioral structure, however, the individual should be capable of the same behavior, which would render the distinction between the contextual and the individual virtually meaningless. This also indicates that the contextual is not a uniquely Japanese phenomenon but a form of human existence that might be found in any culture in the world.

Simmel on Socializing

Simmel's *Grundfragen der Soziologie: Individuum und Gesellschaft* (Basic problems of sociology: individual and society) offers some valuable clues to solving this problem. As its subtitle suggests, this work examines the fundamental relationship between the individual and society, focusing on the essential nature of society and simultaneously providing excellent philosophical observations on human socializing. According to Simmel, society is the sum total of relations among human beings; whatever society's purpose may be, it is essentially the interaction of people. This being the case, society in its pure form consists of interpersonal relations entered into without regard to purpose, that is, the socializing that takes place in a salon.

Simmel's basic stance is what is known as formal sociology. The term "formal" implies that society and the individual are not considered to be entities that exist naturally: The interaction that links people exists first; society is the aggregate of dynamic actions of this sort, and the individual is merely the name given to the point of contact where these actions intermingle. The individual is the composite of a variety of natural qualities and historical causes, and society is the crystallization of life motion, that is, advantages and disadvantages, likes and dislikes, and coincidental encounters; as entities, both the individual and society are merely temporarily unified bodies. To elaborate further, it is not *Gesellschaft* (society) that exists but the eternally fluid process of *Gesellschaftung* (socialization), and scholarship should address not the question of the structural elements of society but that of the "form" in which socialization is manifested.

Obviously people get together and form relationships not for the sake of creating society but for some specific purposes, be it production or war, so social relationships could be regarded as simply the form in which this behavior materializes. To produce goods efficiently, people get together and adopt the form known as the division of labor; this form does not ordinarily appear simply for its own sake. The life of a human being is generally an ongoing process of self-realization that is manifested as political, economic, or religious activity. These seek form in the social system, not the reverse—society is not a preexisting entity that generates various kinds of behavior.

Thus everyday life offers no opportunity to see society in its pure state and no place to experience unadorned interpersonal relations. According to Simmel, however, the one exception is socializing, human interaction for the sole purpose of pleasure, or what might be called the theatrical conversation of the salon, which is liberated from the impulses, concerns, and objectives that constitute the realities of everyday life.

In the world of practical realities, people maintain harmony with others to fight against a third party and talk to one another to convey information. In the context of socializing, however, such practical objectives are set aside: People act harmoniously for the sake of harmony and engage in conversation for the intrinsic pleasure it affords. The social interaction that takes place is an end in itself—in other words, the form of socialization is manifested in its pure state. Not only are vulgar objectives like material gain or power rejected, various internal impulses and tendencies that are part of the individual's basic makeup are also suppressed.

Socializing demands a two-way exchange of action between people so that the individual is not allowed unlimited self-expression, even though the emotions or thoughts may be sincere. In the conversation of the salon, the individual is not only prohibited from making political statements and talking business but also expected to exercise a certain degree of discretion in expressing feelings or asserting an outlook on life, as well as in dress and deportment.

That is, society reveals its original form, while the individual conceals its essential nature and behaves in the form of an individual. Even as the individual behaves in what appears to be a very individualistic fashion, it is actually following the etiquette and conventions of the salon, playing a role dictated by the gathering. By attiring themselves distinctively, people heighten the overall effect of a dance party, and by transforming sexual attractiveness into coquetry they make even romance open to the salon as a whole. As soon as the practical affairs of life are excluded, the individual is able to maintain its unique unity and at the same time become an organic part of the whole, establishing a model of the ideal state of human society.

Simmel's theory bears on this analysis in two respects. First, it contains the germ of the holon concept in that it does not see the closed individual as an absolute but instead considers harmony between the individual and society to be the original state of humankind. Like Tocqueville and

Durkheim, Simmel sees harmony between the self and others as the essential human state and views confrontation between the unprotected individual and the total society as merely one manifestation of socialization. From this it is obvious that neither individualism in the narrow sense nor sociological reductionism are as generally accepted in Western thought as people have assumed, and that criticism of both theories is nothing new. Although the term "contextual" is not used, a concept close to contextualism has long existed in the West, and a state of human existence resembling the contextual—and the value of this state— were widely recognized in the early modern period.

The second point of interest in Simmel's theory is its focus on the behavioral pattern known as socializing, which is considered the pure form of the phenomenon of socialization and the driving force that makes the individual a holonistic entity. On this point Simmel deviates from contextual theory and also from Tocqueville and Durkheim in that he does not have unquestioning faith in the small group as an organization. In other words, the individual's sense of belonging to the small group or feelings of closeness to and degree of dependence on other individuals within it do not, in his view, answer the question of what type of behavior qualifies a human to be a holon of society.

On the contrary, Simmel feels that socializing is destroyed by the individual's need for emotional dependence on or philosophical unity with the group. He regards such acts as just another kind of individual self-assertion that upsets the balance of interaction between the self and others. To keep socializing on a sound footing, the individual is enjoined to exercise a certain discretion even with respect to loyalty to the group. It is essential that the relationship between the self and others be recognized as the essence of life, but this is not a question of direct attentiveness to others or of the quality of feelings. The definitive element is the attitude taken toward behavior that occurs before a person meets with others, the attitude taken toward the person's own behavior. It is, in short, the adoption of an aesthetic attitude regardless of the behavioral specifics involved.

Simmel sees forces inimical to socializing in political, economic, and religious aspirations and in the individual's urge to lay bare the inner self, that is, the attitude characterizing behavior that tries to accomplish something directly. This attitude considers the achievement of goals to be of overriding importance and, when operating unilaterally, makes the actor closed and exclusive, even if it is a small group. Conversely, when this attitude is suppressed, cooperation with others becomes possible even when the individual is the actor, thereby paving the way for the harmony of society as a whole. This second state of human existence is what might be termed the contextual, and it is created not by a specific cultural disposition or climate but, in general, by rejecting the supremacy of goal attainment in favor of more liberal and broad-minded behavior that is not dominated by this attitude.

Socializing and the Gentle Individual

Simmel's theory also contains a few weaknesses that must be shored up before it can be used as a satisfactory alternative to contextualism. The most bothersome is his use of the philosophical terms "form" and "content," which he somewhat rashly seems to liken to the shell and filling of a pie. "Form" usually refers to the state in which something exists, meaning that form cannot appear without content. Just as the form of a plank or a nail cannot exist without wood or steel, the form of society is not viable without substance. Even assuming that society is the form of human behavior, society could not conceivably be established for the sake of behavior that has absolutely no purpose or content. Granted that a social salon differs fundamentally from a political party, a business organization, or a religious group, calling it a manifestation of society in its pure form is incomprehensible, even from a theoretical standpoint.

What is more, the salon is not a gathering simply for the sake of getting together, completely divorced from practical objectives. Although congeniality is closely associated with socializing, congeniality is an effect created by socializing, not its purpose. People bring more practical, defined goals to the salon. Their immediate aims are selected from a broad spectrum of situations in everyday life, ranging from enjoying eating and drinking, games, or sports, through savoring music or theater, down to participating in reading circles or social welfare activities. At times political support groups, businesspeople's organizations, or religious associations turn into salons, transforming even serious, purpose-oriented groups into forums for playful conversation.

The psychological function operating here might be called "creating pretexts": People having a practical objective use it as an excuse for deriving enjoyment from the process of achieving it. This does not disqualify the goal as a goal, because it is to be accomplished in the end, but its ability to dominate the behavioral process is clearly diminished. At the least, people stop rushing to achieve their purpose and are liberated from the state of being so driven by their goals that they become unmindful of themselves.

Liberation from "forgetting oneself" is the definitive criterion of all human enjoyment, all pleasure that is of high cultural quality. Forgetting oneself means becoming so absorbed in an activity that one neglects appearances or, to put it more abstractly, transforms oneself into a means for achieving a goal. When people are absorbed in an immediate objective, whether it is the production of goods or consumption that meets low-level physiological needs, they forget their own existence. It is desirable that a person become an unresisting implement when producing something; and the appearance of someone intently gorging food, for example, is obviously not visible to that person. In either case, the person acts in a dimension so close to the self that it is impossible to see the self objectively. The situation changes completely, however, when it comes to pleasure on a somewhat higher level or consumer activity of a cultural nature.

I have discussed this in detail in my book *Yawarakai kojinshugi no tanjō* (The birth of gentle individualism), but to sum up my main point briefly: A deep experience of anything always means a confirmation of the self. The simplest example is when people want to enjoy the flavor of food; appreciating it deeply clearly means that their attitude passes through two stages.

The initial stage is that of simple physiological pleasure,

in which people are oblivious of the self, intent on rushing ahead to increase their satisfaction quantitatively. Their attitude is a kind of efficiency orientation that actually resembles the approach to production more than to consumption, but people frequently fail to realize this, gorging themselves in their desire for the satisfaction of more food faster. This naive pleasure seeking is, however, soon brought to an end by a paradoxical internal mechanism that eventually brings about a transition to the next stage. Not only appetite for food but all sensual desires reach a limit beyond which satisfaction becomes satiation and pleasure turns into discomfort.

People who realize this naturally stop trying to increase satisfaction quantitatively, aiming instead to postpone satiation and prolong the pleasure. In doing so they extricate consumption from the efficiency-oriented approach to achieving satisfaction, raising it for the first time to the level of pure consumption that is truly capable of providing an alternative to the efficiency-oriented approach that production imposes on life. In concrete terms, this means experiencing the same pleasure in duplicate. In other words, while savoring food, people simultaneously confirm the state of enjoying that food, which they experience as happiness. This might be regarded as relishing the satisfaction of satisfaction.

In other words, the significance of the purpose and the process of consumption is reversed. Most worthy of note here is that in this stage the self as actor with respect to satisfaction splits in two: One self is absorbed in pleasure, while the other self confirms this and experiences happiness. Naturally these two selves are mutually dependent, not antagonistic. The latter is able to experience happiness by virtue of the existence of the former, while the former, confirmed by the latter, is encouraged by its approval and feels more at ease in experiencing pleasure. Two selves are established within one individual and, out of mutual necessity, create a cooperative relationship. In my view, this is the seed of all relations between the self and others that occur in socializing.

Obviously, the individual who seeks a second self for the sake of the satisfaction of the self eventually desires real others as an extension of the self to reinforce the confirmation of its satisfaction. People know that dining with others allows them to savor the food more deeply and prefer this to eating alone because their own happiness is confirmed by a number of others. Moreover, the restraint that Simmel tells us is demanded in socializing enables the individual to avoid excessive absorption in primary pleasure, thereby assuring the leeway to confirm secondary happiness. Viewed from this perspective, when socializing, the individual appears to suppress the self in order to benefit the self and seeks others for the sake of the self. Only in socializing situations is the holonistic harmony of the individual being and the whole guaranteed. This approach also gives us an answer to the second question raised by Simmel, that of why human beings actively desire to socialize.

Simmel made no attempt to delve into the reasons human beings seek to get together, even when practical advantages are set aside, for the enjoyment of pure interaction. He merely proposed the vague concept of a human socializing instinct. I, however, see socializing as one pattern by which the individual seeks to fulfill its desires, a pattern of egocentric behavior on the part of the individual that, by virtue of its egocentricity, also entails respect for others. Socializing has been viewed as a paradoxical manifestation of the phenomenon of human individuation, as discussed earlier. In other words, socializing has been seen as an example of extreme individuation that paradoxically splits up the individual, thereby causing it to turn full cycle and reintegrate once more. Expressed in terms of contextual theory, the contextual is not created on the basis of the negation or amelioration of individualism in the broad sense but comes into being through the paradoxical turnabout that occurs when individualism is taken to its logical conclusion.

This approach makes it possible to go beyond Simmel and see socializing and practically oriented behavior as belonging to a continuum rather than being in conflict. Because the question becomes one of the relationship between the goals and processes of behavior—that is, differences in the attitudes with which goals are pursued—rather than of conflict between form and content, it becomes possible to think in terms of a gradual transition between two poles. For example, between pure socializing and pure politics can be found every conceivable degree of politically motivated socializing and of political activity undertaken with the attitudes characteristic of socializing.

In point of fact, the Confucian political thought of ancient China prescribed that society be governed by means of etiquette, or the rules of socializing, rather than by law. Influenced by China, Japanese politics from the Heian period (794–1192) through the end of the Edo period (1603–1868) was most probably conducted with a more thoroughgoing attitude of socializing than it was in China itself. Not only

149

the seasonal ceremonies and daily etiquette of the imperial court but also the courtesies and pastimes of warrior society were in some ways controlled more by a system of etiquette imposed on people's behavior than they were by law. In some respects the social order of so-called *ie* society was, to be sure, sustained by what Francis L. K. Hsu calls the kin-tract principle; but it was equally underwritten by the etiquette of the tea ceremony and awareness of the norms of the *renga*, or linked verse, gathering. These traditions have been unconsciously carried over into modern times and may be built into what is popularly termed Japanese-style management in the form of the fraternizing that takes place among a company's employees.

History is not governed by laws and is not moved by any single principle. Neither individuation nor the return to reintegration constitutes the only force that moves history; both are affected by the great variety of other elements that go into creating historical realities. Thus it is impossible to use historical laws as a framework for considering what specific form is feasible for the balance between the two. Today, however, as the twentieth century draws to a close, it is clear that modern individualism has grown overripe and, in industrially advanced nations at least, is imperiling the balance vital to culture.

Excessive individualism has now isolated people, making individual self-assertions violent and reinforcing social discord. The greatest problem, however, is that it has made the modern individual an actor who produces—an actor devoted entirely to the attainment of goals who mechanically turns everything into a means. In modern times, freedom means freedom of the will, and freedom of the will implies freedom to plan the future. But for the sake of this freedom, the modern individual transforms the present into a vehicle for achieving the future, converting both itself and other people into tools and rushing through life in pursuit of goals. As a result, modern people are constantly postponing gratification in life, depriving themselves of a place where they can truly live the present, and suffering from loss of the feeling that life is worth living.

The solution to this problem, as already implied repeatedly, lies in the revival of pure consumption through a return to socializing. I have named the human image that should be recovered the "gentle individual," which most emphatically needs to be distinguished from the "rugged individual" of modern individualism. I stress once more, however, that the gentle individual is very much an individual and, depending on the thoroughness of individuation, may be even more individualistic than the rugged individual. Having confirmed this fact gives me even greater confidence in the possibility of the gentle individual's materializing, because no matter what problems arise in a given stage of individualism, they can be overcome not by groupism but by further progress in individuation.

Notes

1. The labels applied to the periods of Japanese history may follow any of a number of systems depending on the perspective and objectives of the historiographer. The most commonly used divisions, which derive their names from the successive geographical seats of political authority, correspond approximately to changes in the nature of the authority that governed the country. Thus the Nara period (710–94) saw ancient emperors exercising direct rule. The Heian period (794–1192) refers to the centuries when aristocratic families, most notably the Fujiwara regents, controlled the country from the Heian capital (present-day Kyoto). The Kamakura period (1192–1333) opened with warrior hegemons assuming virtual control of the government. Rival factions in both the imperial family and the warrior clans marked the strife-ridden period of the Northern and Southern Courts (1333–92). Another warrior regime, based this time in the Muromachi section of Kyoto, presided over the ensuing Muromachi period (1392–1573). The years of de facto rule by Toyotomi Hideyoshi are called the Momoyama period (1573–1603) after the district of Kyoto where he built his castle. Similarly, the Edo period (1603–1868) was launched when the seat of a new warrior administration was moved to Edo (present-day Tokyo). Depending on the focus of interest, these periods may be further broken down: Art history, for example, divides the Heian period into Early Heian and Late Heian and distinguishes the Kitayama and Higashiyama eras within the Muromachi period.

Another type of periodization marks off the country's history in larger segments: *genshi*, covering the prehistoric periods; *kodai*, the ancient era, which roughly corresponds to the Nara and Heian periods; *chūsei*, the medieval period, referring broadly to the era extending from the late Heian through the Muromachi periods; *kinsei*, from the Momoyama through the Edo periods; *kindai*, the early modern age of industrialization that began at the end of the nineteenth century; and *gendai*, literally meaning "the present age" but probably better translated as "late modern," covering the latter half of the twentieth century. Although historians are still arguing over precisely when each begins and ends, the use of these divisions is widely accepted. Originally derived from Western historiography, the way this type of periodization is used by the Japanese attests to their distinctive sense of history.

In brief, *kinsei*, the era before Japan had full-scale contact with the West, can be seen as a time of spontaneous, indigenous preparation for modernization. *Kinsei* is generally considered to begin when military control of the country fell to Hideyoshi, who undertook a nationwide cadastral survey to serve as a basis for levying taxes, introduced a unified system of weights and measures, and laid down laws governing the class system. He separated peasants and warriors into distinct social classes, forbidding the former to own weapons and requiring the latter to leave rural villages and live in towns. The towns that thus became the seats of local territorial lords developed rapidly, strengthening the foundations for trade and handicraft industries. With the entire country under the administrative control of the semi-feudal, semi-bureaucratic central government in Edo, the erstwhile territorial warlords became military bureaucrats who, along with the merchants, directed their energies to developing many kinds of local industries throughout the country. This enabled Japan to accumulate the capital needed for modernization and succeed in the domestic production of cotton, sugar, and other important products that would otherwise have had to be imported.

The term *kinsei* came into use among Japanese historians relatively early and was firmly established in the society at large by the Taishō period (1912–26). The first volume of Tokutomi Sohō's 100-volume *Kinsei Nihon kokumin shi* (The history of the Japanese people during *kinsei*) appeared in 1918. At the time, the common wisdom held that Japan's modernization had begun due to Western influence and everything prior to 1868 was "feudalistic." Despite this, however, the prevalence of the term *kinsei* indicates that the Japanese were already distinguishing this period from the earlier *chūsei*, if only subconsciously. But not until after World War II did people begin to assert openly that Japan's modernization owed much to indigenous factors that already existed embryonically in the Edo period.

The distinction between *kindai* and *gendai* is of relatively recent origin, appearing after World War II. *Gendai*, which is considered to begin around the time of the war, includes surrealistic, abstract and subsequent art forms, music since the introduction of the twelve-tone scale, and existentialism and ensuing philosophies. In reference to general social phenomena, however, this term is used very loosely, and during the past half century it has been fashionable to apply the *gendai* label to every new social development, distinguishing it from whatever is considered to have characterized *kindai*.

This probably relates to the progressivist atmosphere of postwar Japan that had people living in constant expectation of innovation. It may also relate, however, to the ambivalence with which the Japanese have long viewed the rapid modernization and overly impetuous industrialization that has been in process since the Meiji period (1868–1912). *Kindai* in the narrow sense—an age of machines and smoke, division of labor and groups—has always been seen as a transitional process that would eventually come to an end. This ambivalence has made postindustrial theories attractive to the Japanese and may have led to their being more readily accepted in Japan than elsewhere.

2. Honesty in the sense of not lying and not deceiving others is, of course, an eternal and universal human ethic. Ancient societies, however, did not differentiate honesty from loyalty. Within the family, village, or clan, loyalty and honesty meant both not betraying the group's interests and not deceiving one's fellows. Moral worth was determined on the basis of the externally visible results of action, and nobody questioned the feelings of an individual who sacrificed self for lord or family. In other words, no distinction was made between the individual's internal world and external behavior, so the question of consistency between feeling and action was never consciously formulated.

The concept of honesty as it was used from the Muromachi through the Edo periods clearly differed qualitatively from earlier ethics. Suzuki Shōzō's *Mōanjō* is worth particular attention because he clearly differentiated sincerity from loyalty and filial piety. To these traditional ethical concepts he added *makoto* (or *seijitsu*), which he used in the sense of being true to oneself, of conformity between a person's inner feelings and external actions. Regarding people's fondness for children, too, he distinguished between superficial kindness and true affection, stressing that the latter is real love.

Even in the West, this kind of internal sincerity has been brought into question and made a central ethical precept only since the seventeenth century. According to Lionel Trilling's *Sincerity and Authenticity*, Shakespeare made one of the earliest statements of this concept in *Hamlet*, when he had Polonius admonish his son, "To thine own self be true, And it must follow as the night the day, Thou canst not then be false to any man." Hamlet, ever conscious of the inconsistency between his feelings and actions, is anguished by the greater strength of his feelings. Trilling explains that the true self that was discovered in this era conflicted with the ethics of the public realm, making modern Western history an ongoing struggle between honesty and loyalty.

Japanese of the Edo period were conscious of the conflict between these moral principles, making the clash between *giri* and *ninjō*, duty and human feeling, the main theme of kabuki and bunraku plays. In many of these dramas, the leading figures suffered over whether to be true to their own feelings and live for romantic or familial love or to sacrifice these in the name of social ethics or loyalty to a lord. Solving the dilemma through suicide, particularly lovers' double suicide, is a denouement found throughout Chikamatsu Monzaemon's leading works. In the past, critics have viewed these double suicides as defeatist behavior on the part of "feudalistic people," but in terms of motivation, at least, this drastic solution should be seen as the expression of a modern awareness of the self and the need to be faithful to it.

3. Robert N. Bellah, *Tokugawa Religion* (Boston: Beacon Press, 1970), p. 158.

4. Donald Keene, trans., *Four Major Plays of Chikamatsu* (New York: Columbia University Press, 1964), pp. 151–52.

5. *Essays in Idleness*, trans. Donald Keene (Tokyo: Charles E. Tuttle Co., 1981), pp. 118–19.

6. Kato Shuichi, *A History of Japanese Literature*, trans. David Chibbett (Tokyo: Kodansha International Ltd., 1981) vol. 1, p. 285.

7. A multilayered aesthetic structure, or a paradoxical structure of artistic expression, is one of Japanese culture's most important characteristics. An aesthetic approach that gave rise to categories like *yūgen* and *wabi*, this overlapping structure appeared most prominently from the Muromachi through the Edo periods, but it stemmed from a much longer aesthetic tradition. From antiquity the Japanese have held beauty to be a worldly value, regarding artistic expression as action that people take with respect to other people.

In his preface to the *Kokinshū* (Collection of ancient and modern poetry), the tenth century poet Ki no Tsurayuki (884–946) wrote that Japanese poetry originates in the human heart, stirring people's feelings, and moving the natural and the supernatural, spirits and gods. As a young scholar, Donald Keene was to express his astonishment at Tsurayuki's words in *Japanese Literature: An Introduction for Western Readers* (1955). Tsurayuki's contemporaries in the Western world held a perspective that was the direct opposite of this, for they believed that literature was the product of a supernatural power that dwelt in the spirits of humans and inspired them to compose it. From the age of the ancient Greeks, beauty was considered by Westerners to be either the imitation of an ideal (or the imitation of an imitation of an ideal) or something created by the genius that a transcendental power bestowed on humans (Friedrich W. J. Schelling's "die Gunst der Natur"). Discovering beauty was akin to knowing truth, and the artist, like the priest, was closer to the transcendental than ordinary people. The artist's work was likened to divine creation, and the artist was expected to be isolated from the profane world of ordinary mortals. In Western aesthetics, the audience's acceptance of a work was secondary, considered at best to be merely a fictive experience of the process of artistic creation.

For the Japanese, however, poetry has been the product of social situations since at least the eighth century *Man'yōshū*. Through the ages a prodigious number of poems have been composed as entertainment at parties or as presents included in letters. In the tenth century, gatherings were held at the court for the express purpose of composing poems, which were recited, evaluated, and singled out for honor (a custom that is still carried on by the imperial court). Out of this milieu was born a new poetic form, the *renga*, which involved a number of poets getting together to link their individual verses in a single poem. Japanese poets and artists are certainly not lonely figures, and the audience is seen as assisting the act of creation. Tales in prose were recited in the streets and in social salons, and paintings were made the subject of appreciative conversation at tea ceremonies. Muromachi scroll paintings literally incorporated the act of appreciation into the creative process: The viewer expressed observations on the painting in poetic form, and the work was completed by inscribing this poem on the painting. The tea ceremony is the quintessence of aesthetics uniting with socializing: The act of getting together to share tea and conversation has, as a whole, been elevated into an art form.

Art that is essentially an expression of divine favor and created for the eyes of a transcendental power strives for pure and consummate beauty. In the West, elegance and sublimity, realism and grotesque beauty all strive for an ultimate ideal. But beauty that is basically a product of the human heart, that has been created for human eyes, cannot strive for extreme purity. Unlike divine eyes, human senses tire easily and are unable to withstand excessive stimulation. Overdoses of the sumptuous or the sweet satiate people and eventually cause them distress. Moreover, people are highly jealous of others' self-expression and detect overt displays of the ego in expression that is too overwhelming. When the excessively grand or ingeniously minute is presented as evidence of human ability, the viewer senses the smug attitude of the creator in the background and finds it distasteful.

The overlapping structure of Japanese aesthetics can be considered a kind of strategy to cope with such subtleties of human psychology. It acts as a filter to soften excessive stimulation of the senses and as a gesture of self-restraint on the part of the person creating the expression. *Wabi*, *yūgen*, and other aesthetic concepts evolving from this milieu are not, however, totally unrelated to the ethereal and the religious. The Japanese are fully sensitive to values transcending what is worldly and are quite capable of perceiving the sacred in the beautiful. But because Japanese artists start out with relationships between humans, for them to arrive at the transcendental means traversing the reverse path of that taken by Western artists. In other words, the Japanese initially exercise discretion in expressing the self out of fear of specific other people; this fear is next directed toward all of human society, then further extended to the world as a whole, including natural phenomena. Beyond this are found gods and buddhas, in the face of which the artist endeavors to suppress overt displays of the ego.

8. Ryusaku Tsunoda, Wm. Theodore De Bary, and Donald Keene, comps., *Sources of Japanese Tradition* (New York: Columbia University Press, 1958), p. 349.

9. Ibid., p. 347.

Bibliography

Hamaguchi Esyun, Kumon Shumpei. *Nihonteki shūdan shugi* (Japanese groupism). Tokyo: Yūhikaku, 1982.

Hayashiya Tatsusaburō. *Suminokura Soan*. Tokyo: Asahi Shimbun Sha, 1978.

Hsu, Francis L. K. *Iemoto: The Heart of Japan*. Cambridge, Mass.: Schenkman Publishing Company, 1975.

Lipnack, Jessica and Stamps, Jeffrey. *Networking*. New York: Doubleday & Company, Inc., 1982.

Masaki Tokuzō. *Hon'ami gyōjōki to Kōetsu* (The Hon'ami diary and Kōetsu). Tokyo: Chūō Kōron Bijutsu Shuppansha, 1981.

Matsuki Hiroshi. *Tsutaya Jūzaburō*. Tokyo: Nihon Keizai Shimbun Sha, 1988.

Moriya Takeshi. *Genroku bunka* (Genroku culture). Tokyo: Kōbundō, 1987.

Murakami Yasusuke, Kumon Shumpei, Satō Seizaburō. *Bunmei to shite no ie shakai* (Ie society as a civilization). Tokyo: Chūō Kōron Sha, 1979.

Nakao Sasuke. *Hana to ki no bunkashi* (The cultural history of flowers and trees). Tokyo: Iwanami Shoten, 1986.

Suzuki Shōzō dōjin zenshū (The collected writings of Suzuki Shōzō). Edited by Suzuki Tesshin. Tokyo: Sankibō, 1962.

Tanaka Yūko. *Edo no sōzōryoku* (Creativity in the Edo period). Tokyo: Chikuma Shobō, 1986.

Tsukuba Hisaharu. *Nihon no nōsho* (Handbooks of agronomy in Japan). Tokyo: Chūō Kōron Sha, 1987.

Tsunoyama Sakae. *Tokei no shakaishi* (The social history of clocks). Tokyo: Chūō Kōron Sha, 1984.

Yamamoto Shichihei. *Nihon shihon shugi no seishin* (The spirit of Japanese capitalism). Tokyo: Kōbun Sha, 1984.

Yamazaki Masakazu. *Yawarakai kojinshugi no tanjō* (The birth of gentle individualism). Tokyo: Chūō Kōron Sha, 1984.

Index